# Blessed

## FIRST COMMUNION

**Dynamic Catholic**
Be Bold. Be Catholic®

# My name is

_____ .

I am blessed, and God made me wonderfully
and marvelously in his own image.
Jesus wants me to become
the-best-version-of-myself,
grow in virtue, and live a holy life.

# On this date

_____

I am going to receive the incredible gift of Jesus
during my First Communion.
I am truly blessed.

# Table of Contents

# Welcome!

One of the most incredible gifts God has given us as human beings is the ability to dream. Unlike any other creature, we can look into the future, imagine something bigger and better, and then come back into the present and work to bring about that richly imagined better future.

Imagine how the Church would be different if children, teenagers, and young adults wanted to attend Mass each Sunday. Imagine how the Church would be different if every Catholic in America had a dynamic personal relationship with God, believed in the true presence of Jesus in the Eucharist, and made daily prayer a touchstone in their lives. Preparation for First Communion presents the perfect opportunity to turn this dream into a reality.

Catechesis is the Church's efforts to bring to life the teachings of Jesus Christ in the lives of ordinary men, women, and children. Religious education classes are one of the primary forms of catechesis.

But evangelization precedes catechesis.

Evangelization is first and foremost a dialogue. It is not a monologue. Evangelization is a personal and powerful conversation that leads to conversion of heart, mind, and soul.

And let's face it, our young people need to encounter the living God. They need to hear the Gospel in a way that is personal, intriguing, relevant, compelling, and attractive. They need to know that they are not alone in the journey of life, they need to know that they are blessed to be sons or daughters of a great King, and they need to know that God will never abandon them.

It is our hope that this program will not only prepare young Catholics for their First Communion in a dynamic way, but that it will inspire them to become lifelong Catholics.

These materials are the result of thousands of hours of rigorous research, development, and testing. More than 500 people have been involved in the process. Throughout the development of the program, students, catechists, teachers, DREs, parents, and pastors have told us what is working and what isn't. Over and over, we have refined our offering based on their feedback.

And we are not finished yet. For decades, children have been using programs that were developed once and never changed, or changed every seven years. This won't be the case with *Blessed*. We hope you provide feedback so that we can continue to improve this offering regularly.

Thank you for being part of this journey. We realize that the role you play in preparing young Catholics for First Communion may be a thankless one—so we want to say thank you. Thank you for everything that you are doing for the Church. It is our hope and prayer that the program will make your experience with today's young Catholics deeply fulfilling for you and for them.

There are moments when a child's eyes become wide with excitement and begin to sparkle. At Dynamic Catholic we refer to this as the "I get it now" moment. May our efforts combined with your dedication produce more "I get it now" moments in the eyes of your students this year!

May the grace of our abundantly generous God inspire you and give you courage, wisdom, and patience.

The Dynamic Catholic Team

# *the* Dynamic Catholic Approach

Blessed *is different. One look at the materials and that is clear. It looks different and feels different because it is different. The way we developed the program is very different from how Catholic programs have been developed in the past. Backed by rigorous research and testing, Blessed has harnessed the latest and most effective technology in the world to create an unforgettable experience.*

Blessed *isn't different just for the sake of being different. The old way just isn't working. Eighty-five percent of young Catholics stop practicing their faith within ten years of their Confirmation. The stakes are too high. Different is needed.*

# The Process

What do you remember about your First Communion? Most people can't remember anything. Together we can change that for the next generation of Catholics.

There are many programs that faithfully present the teachings of the Church. But that alone is not enough. While presenting the Church's teachings faithfully is essential, it is also critical that they be presented in ways that are engaging, accessible, and relevant.

So we set out to create the very best First Communion program in the world—the most dynamic program to prepare children for this great Catholic Moment. As a result, *Blessed* has taken more than three years to develop. This is what it took to create the world-class program you now hold in your hands.

### YEAR ONE: LISTEN

We spent an entire year just listening: meetings—hundreds of meetings—focus groups, and phone calls. Catechists, teachers, parents, DREs, and priests told us they wanted engaging workbooks, catechist-friendly leader guides, resources that draw the parents into the process, and powerful music. They told us it would be nice if for once, our Catholic materials were as good as the secular programs our children experience every day. But most of all they wanted programs that help their children discover the genius of Catholicism in a way that inspires them to become lifelong Catholics.

### YEAR TWO: EXPLORE

We spent the second year exploring every First Communion preparation program that was currently available. We analyzed the differences and similarities among these programs. We investigated which parts of each were effective and which aspects simply weren't working. We also explored best practices among other Christian churches and groups to discover how they were engaging their students. Then we spent a lot of time asking why: Why does this work? Why doesn't this work? Why don't children respond to this or that? And finally we asked: What will it take to really engage them in a meaningful discussion about the genius of Catholicism?

By the third year we were developing our own program based on what we had learned. This began a cycle of developing and testing. We would develop snippets of material and then test them with experts. A lot of the material worked, but some of it didn't. And all of it was improved by the feedback we got during testing.

Now it is time to share *Blessed* with the world. But we see this as a larger pilot study. We know it isn't perfect; no program is. The difference is, we are not done yet. Many programs get launched and are never changed. But we are excited to continuously improve this program based on the feedback you and your children provide to us. So if you see a typo or a substantial way to improve this program, please let us know.

# The Experience

*Blessed* is a Dynamic Catholic Experience designed to prepare young Catholics for the Sacrament of First Communion.

At the heart of the program are 42 short animated films, which range in length from 1 to 15 minutes.

Here is a quick look at the different ways *Blessed* can be experienced:

 **Online**: The entire program is available online to anyone at any time.

 **Hard Copies**: The workbook, leader guide, and DVD series will also be available as hard copies for parishes and individuals who prefer them.

**3** **Audiobook**: For any Catholic in America to experience the universally informative and inspiring content of *Blessed*, it is perfect for parents and loved ones of those preparing for the Sacrament.

**4** **Music CD**: Catchy and inspiring music for use in the car, classroom, and home.

 **Content in Spanish**: The entire program will also be available in Spanish.

# Children ...

- Have great differences in size and abilities

- Love talking, often exaggerating stories

- Work hard to please parents, catechists, teachers, and other adults

- Thrive with structure and routine

- Are sensitive to adult assessment

- Compare themselves to others

- Place high importance on friendships

- View things as right or wrong, wonderful or terrible, with very little middle ground or gray area

- Are beginning to use logical reasoning

- Have a tendency to make decisions based on influence of others

- Have difficulty with abstract reasoning

- Need closure and desire to finish assignments

- Want work to be perfect, erasing constantly

- Desire to work slowly

- Collect and organize things

- Learn best when they feel an emotional connection

- Have a strong sense of wonder

*Typically, children receive the Sacraments of First Reconciliation and First Communion in the second grade. But, we think you will agree, *Blessed* is for every Catholic in America.

## The Elements

At Dynamic Catholic we believe everything we do as Catholics should be excellent. That's why we have sought out the best resources in the world to create an unforgettable experience with the genius of Catholicism.

### THE WORKBOOKS

The beautifully illustrated workbooks are made up of more than 250 hand-painted works of art by an internationally acclaimed artist. The combination of rich visuals and dynamic content brings the faith to life for children more than ever before. The content meets children where they are and leads them step-by-step to where God is calling them to be.

### THE PARENT COMPONENT

The *Blessed* parent email program, audiobook, and music CD are an answer to what catechists, teachers, DREs, priests, and Bishops have been crying out for: a dynamic way to engage disengaged parents and encourage them to make faith a priority in their lives.

### THE ANIMATION

Our research revealed that cognitive retention in children from ages 6 to 9 is directly linked to emotional connection, and nothing connects with children on a significant emotional level quite like animation. So we thought it was time for Catholics to harness the techniques Disney has been using for more than ninety years to influence our children.

We teamed up with an Emmy Award–winning animation studio to create the first ever animated film series for sacramental preparation. Each of the 42 episodes will engage your children's sense of wonder and take them on an unforgettable adventure into the story of Jesus and the life-giving truths of his Church.

## The Format

This program is divided into six sessions. Each session has at least 60 minutes of classroom material that can be utilized as a catechist sees fit for a particular group of students. The sessions are broken up in a way that the content can be shortened per class over a longer period of time or lengthened over a shorter period of time.

**Our research revealed that cognitive retention in children from ages 6 to 9 is directly linked to emotional connection, and nothing connects with children on a significant emotional level quite like animation.**

## THE SESSIONS

Each of the six sessions in *Blessed* have many layers. As you plan out your teaching time, look ahead, and plan for this type of structure:

**①** **Opening Prayer**

**②** **Teachable Moments**: Episodes 2, 3, 4, and 6 are the episodes with the primary teaching content.

**③** **From the Bible**: Every Episode 5 will utilize Holy Scripture to illustrate the primary point of the session. This will help Scripture come to life!

**④** **Show What You Know**: Here is an opportunity for students to answer true-or-false and fill-in-the-blank questions so you can gauge how well they are grasping the material.

**⑤** **Journal with Jesus**: This is a prayerful opportunity for students to have an intimate conversation with Jesus. They can write or draw their thoughts to Jesus.

**⑥** **Closing Prayer**

Additionally, there are two features intended to streamline and enhance the teaching experience:

1. Every spread has a step-by-step list of instructions and activities.

2. The page numbers correspond with the student workbook so the two books match one another.

## TIPS

Throughout this leader guide, you will find a variety of tips. We recommend you read all of the tips through, start to finish before each class. This will give you a good sense of how to engage these young Catholics in a dynamic experience. It will also give you confidence and allow you to enjoy the process—and the more you enjoy it, the more they enjoy it! Remember, you are offering them something beautiful. Give them a beautiful encounter with God and his Church and you will change their lives forever. Don't lose sight of that.

## ICONS

 **Prayer Icon**: Indicates a moment when you are encouraged to pray with the children.

 **Read and Explore**: Indicates a suggested time for children to explore the workbooks and for the material to be read aloud, with a partner, or silently.

 **Watch and Discuss**: Indicates a time to watch one, two, or sometimes even three episodes, followed by discussion.

 **Show What You Know**: Indicates when children are asked to complete true-or-false and fill-in-the-blank activities.

 **Journal with Jesus**: Indicates the time when students engage in a personal, guided conversation with Jesus.

 **Time Icon**: Indicates a guide to help you plan approximately how long each activity will take.

## QUOTES

Throughout this book there are quotes from some of the great Christian spiritual champions. May their words provide you with tremendous encouragement and wisdom throughout the process and, most of all, may they inspire you to become the-best-version-of-yourself, grow in virtue, and live a holy life.

# Suggested Formats

One of the great challenges in developing First Communion materials is that each Diocese prepares candidates in different ways for different periods of time, with different class formats. With this in mind, we have developed *Blessed* with a suggested format, but in a way that makes it infinitely flexible.

We suggest that the program be experienced through six 90-minute classes. These can take place once a month for six months, twice a month for three months, or once a week for six weeks.

If this is not how you currently structure First Communion preparation, we invite you to consider trying something new. Just because you have always done it a certain way doesn't mean you need to continue to do it a certain way—especially if that way isn't producing results.

## Other Formats

The core of the program is 42 short animated episodes. In the suggested format, children would experience seven of these short episodes in each class. But you could use one per class for 42 sessions, two per class for twenty-one sessions, or three per class for fourteen sessions.

The program was specifically designed to have this flexibility. Each short episode is content and concept rich. This leads to great opportunities for class or small-group discussions.

Children at this age crave repetition. For those parishes and schools that have longer programs and need more material, don't be afraid to identify key episodes and show them multiple times. There will be certain episodes that the children will gravitate toward; let those episodes and their themes become part of the fabric of the class and ultimately part of the fabric of their lives.

## We Are Praying for You

In Mark's Gospel, just after the Transfiguration, Jesus comes down the mountain with Peter, James, and John. Waiting for Jesus is a father desperate for his son to be healed. The father is a bit frustrated because Jesus' disciples have been unable to rid his son of the demon that plagues him. Jesus rebukes the unclean spirit and it leaves the boy. His disciples, no doubt frustrated by their inability to cure the boy, ask Jesus, "Why could we not cast it out?" Jesus answers them, "This kind can come out only through prayer and fasting" (Mark 9:29).

Some things are so important they need prayer and fasting. In addition to creating *Blessed* we have been praying and fasting for you and the children who will experience this program. Together, with the grace of God, we will transform the hearts of all the children who experience *Blessed*, helping them become all God created them to be.

If there is anything Dynamic Catholic can ever do to serve you, please reach out to our Mission Team at 859-980-7900 or email us at blessed@dynamiccatholic.com.

**Together, with the grace of God, we will transform the hearts of all the children who experience *Blessed*, helping them become all God created them to be.**

**1**

# Sunday is Special

## OBJECTIVES

- **TO PROCLAIM** the Eucharist as one of life's greatest blessings.

- **TO EXPLAIN** that every day is a new day in our journey with God—and every day God has a message he is trying to share with us.

- **TO TEACH** that going to Mass on Sunday is a great way to show God we are grateful for all our blessings.

# • Greet the children at the door.

# • Let the children know they are being prayed for.

## WELCOME

Most of the time, the people God invites to carry out his incredible work are surprised that they have been chosen. There's Moses, a murderer with a speech impediment; Peter, the uneducated fisherman; Mary, a betrothed virgin; Paul, the Christian killer; and Joan of Arc, a peasant girl with no military experience. God truly does work in unexpected ways!

God has chosen you for the special mission of preparing these children for their First Communion. What a wonderful opportunity you have before you!

Thank you for saying yes to this mission. Thank you for bringing children closer to Jesus. Your work makes an eternal difference.

Your first day with these children presents a fabulous opportunity. Most leaders who fail, do so because they believe knowledge is the only tool a teacher needs to effectively lead a class. This could not be farther from the truth. Decades of research reveal that children won't hear a single word you say until they know how much you care about them.

So greet them at the door, tell them you are praying for them, learn their names and favorite movies, and share your own story. Let the children in your class know you care about them and the impact you will have on their lives will last a lifetime.

**Prayer Icon**

**Read and Explore**

**Watch and Discuss**

**Show What You Know**

**Journal with Jesus**

**Time Tracker**

## OPENING PRAYER

### Step-by-Step

**1** Introduce the opening prayer by saying: "Let's take a moment in silence to be still and quiet and open ourselves up to whatever God wants to lead us to today."

**2** Make the Sign of the Cross together deliberately.

**3** Read the opening prayer slowly and reflectively.

**Human labor alone cannot achieve a divine purpose.**

Mustard Seeds

**My Notes:**

_____

_____

_____

_____

_____

_____

_____

# 1
# Sunday is Special

---

God, our loving Father,
thank you for all the ways you bless me.
Help me to be aware that every person,
place, and adventure I experience is an
opportunity to love you more.
Fill me with a desire to change and to grow,
and give me the grace to become
the-best-version-of-myself in
every moment of every day.

Amen.

2 minutes

**tip**
Bring a pack of sticky notes or small index cards or paper that size. Let the kids write down prayer requests as each session begins. Tell them you will take them home each week and pray for their special intentions. Provide a basket for the children to place the prayer requests into. Explain that you will not share them with anyone. But do follow up with the children about them. For example: "How is your grandmother doing?"

**Pray, hope, and don't worry. Worry is useless. God is merciful and will hear your prayer.**

St. Pio of Pietrelcina

## WATCH AND DISCUSS

### Step-by-Step

 **1** Introduce the first episode by saying: "Ben, his sister Sarah, and her pet gerbil Hemingway are ready to enjoy a big feast with five of their friends."

**2** Watch Episode 1.

**Seek out the gentleness within you that encourages people to feel comfortable around you.**

Mustard Seeds

## Keep Counting Your Blessings

Welcome. It is time to set out on another great adventure together.

One of the greatest blessings you will ever experience in this life is the Eucharist. So this journey toward your First Communion is very important.

God is inviting you to a great banquet. You are blessed.

**My Notes:**

_____

_____

_____

_____

_____

_____

_____

You are blessed in so many ways. But every blessing you experience flows from the first blessing. You are a child of God; this is the original blessing.

And now God wants to bless you with the Eucharist!

When you count your blessings before you go to bed tonight, remember to include your favorite foods, the people you love, your talents, your favorite activities and places, and most of all God for giving you all these blessings.

**7 minutes**

**tip**
This is the first animated episode they are going to experience in the program. Make sure everyone can see the screen. When the episode is over, share something specific you liked. For example: "I really like how each of the kids shared something they are grateful for; I love their clubhouse and the tubes set up around the room for the gerbil, Hemingway; I thought it was funny the way Tiny picked Ben up in order to hang the painting"; etc.

**In all created things discern the providence and wisdom of God, and in all things give him thanks.**

St. Teresa of Avila

3

## WATCH AND DISCUSS

**Step-by-Step**

**1** Let they children know the episode they are about to watch is longer than the first one. Suggest they try to get comfortable.

**2** Introduce Episode 2 by setting an important expectation: "In this episode, Sarah goes on a quest to discover why God gives us gifts like First Communion. Let's see what she discovers!"

**3** Watch Episode 2.

**4** Ask the children:"What did Sarah discover, why does God give us great Catholic Moments like First Communion?"

- BECAUSE GOD WANTS US TO LIVE A RICH, FULL HAPPY LIFE IN THIS WORLD—AND LIVE WITH HIM IN HEAVEN IN ETERNAL BLISS FOREVER.

## Your Journey with God Continues

We are continuing our journey with God. So, let's review where we have been and where we are going.

**My Notes:**

_____

_____

_____

_____

_____

_____

_____

# Baptism

Before Jesus began his ministry he visited his cousin, John the Baptist, in the desert. John was baptizing many people in the Jordan River to prepare them for the coming of the Messiah.

John encouraged everyone he met to turn back to God, acknowledge their sin, and seek God's forgiveness.

**14 minutes**

_____
_____
_____
_____
_____
_____
_____

**tip**

If possible, take a moment to write the question on the board or some place everyone can see. This will help the majority of the children in your class who are visual learners. Write the answer on the board too and keep it up there for the entire class. Let the children be reminded of the kind of life God dreams for them.

**Let the little children come to me, and do not hinder them, for the kingdom of God belongs to such as these.**

Matthew 19:14

## READ AND EXPLORE

### Step-by-Step

**1** Invite the children to explore the illustration. Ask them, "What do you see?" Then discuss things they notice. Be prepared to start the conversation with your own answer.

**2** Ask the children: "What do you think John the Baptist felt when he baptized Jesus? *Hint:* John knew Jesus was the Savior."

- AMAZED
- GRATEFUL
- UNWORTHY
- HAPPY

**You are called to be a leader and the only way to lead is with an example of virtue.**

Mustard Seeds

When Jesus arrived at the Jordan River, he asked John to baptize him. At first John refused because he knew that Jesus was the Messiah and, therefore, sinless. But Jesus insisted.

Jesus did not need to be baptized like you and I for the forgiveness of sins, but he wanted to lead by example. He was fully divine but he was also fully human. By allowing himself to be baptized, Jesus demonstrated great love and respect for our humanity.

Each year the Church celebrates Jesus' baptism on the last day of the Christmas season. We celebrate his baptism because it reminds us of all Jesus did so that we could be reasonably happy in this life and happier than we can imagine with him forever in heaven.

Do you know when and where you were baptized? Baptism was the beginning of your new life in Jesus. This is when you became a member of his Church and joined the largest and most famous family in the world. You probably cannot remember your Baptism but it was one of the most powerful moments of your life.

Just as the Church celebrates Jesus' baptism, we should celebrate our own baptism. This year celebrate the day of your Baptism like you do your birthday.

**My Notes:**

_____

_____

_____

_____

_____

_____

_____

2 minutes

**tip**

Some of the children might need a few more questions to get the conversation started. Open-ended questions are a great way to stir their imagination: "What do you see?" or "Why do you think water is coming off Jesus?" or "Does John the Baptist look different than the other people?" If they need a hint, tell the children to look at his clothes. By discussing things they notice, you will open the door to a deeper level of conversation.

**God watched over me before I knew him and before I learned or sensed or even distinguished between good and evil.**

St. Patrick

## READ AND EXPLORE

### Step-by-Step

**1** Invite one student to read each paragraph of the story about Joseph and his brothers.

> You cannot live without dreams. Dreams foster hope, and hope is one of the forces by which men and women live.

The Rhythm of Life

# First Reconciliation

Joseph was one of thirteen children. His older brothers disliked him very much because he had fabulous dreams. One day while he was working out in the fields, Joseph's brothers tricked him and sold him into slavery. He was sent to Egypt and forced to stay there, far from his family and friends.

A few years later, a terrible famine spread through the land and Joseph's family was starving. Egypt was the only country that had prepared for the famine, so the Pharaoh appointed a governor to be in charge of all the food. Joseph's brothers went to Egypt to beg the governor for food. They didn't realize that the governor was Joseph, the brother they had sold into slavery.

**My Notes:**

_____

_____

_____

_____

_____

_____

_____

_____

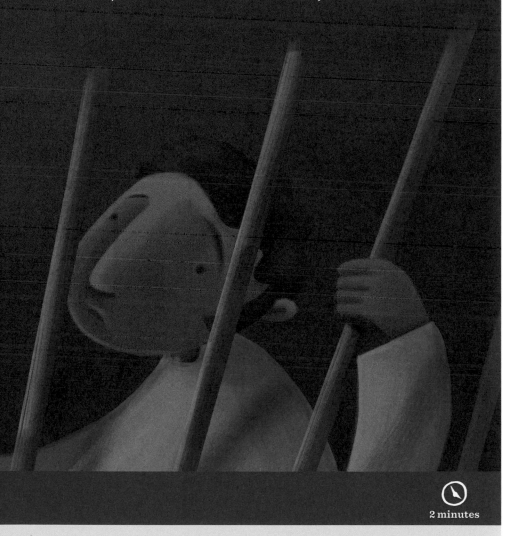

Joseph had a choice to make. He could either hold a grudge against his brothers for being so mean to him or he could choose to forgive them. What would you do? It wouldn't be easy to forgive them. He had suffered so much because of what his brothers had done to him, but Joseph was kind and merciful and chose to forgive them.

When Joseph revealed himself to his brothers they were amazed!

2 minutes

tip

Theodore Roosevelt once wrote, "A thorough knowledge of the Bible is worth more than a college education." Why? Because he knew by experience that the Bible leads us to God's mysterious and fabulous plans for our lives. The Bible isn't just another book and the stories it contains are not just any old stories. The Bible is the guidebook for your life and the lives of the children in your class. It's transformational. If you express reverence and appreciation for the Bible, the impact on the lives of the children will be incalculable.

**Truly I tell you, anyone who will not receive the kingdom of God like a little child will never enter it.**

Mark 10:15

# READ AND EXPLORE

## Step-by-Step

**1** Read the text out loud.

**2** Tell the children a time when you forgave someone who didn't deserve forgiveness or when someone forgave you and you didn't deserve it. Never underestimate the power of conveying humility.

**Confession is a gift. Behold the beauty. Embrace the treasure.**

Rediscover Catholicism

Life can be messy. We all make mistakes and from time to time we all do things that we know we shouldn't. We may not sell our siblings into slavery, but we do offend God and hurt others. We call this sin, and the thing about sin is that it makes us unhappy. Sin separates us from God, and we simply cannot be happy when we are separated from God. Reconciliation reunites us with God and fills us with joy again.

**My Notes:**

_____

_____

_____

_____

_____

_____

_____

When did you receive your First Reconciliation? Your First Reconciliation was a great blessing and it is a blessing you can receive as many times as you wish for the rest of your life. I encourage you to go to Reconciliation and pour your heart out to God anytime you feel far from him. He will give you peace and courage to press on.

2 minutes

**tip**
Whisper or drop your voice off to capture the children's attention. It can be more effective than raising your voice.

**The moments of a sincere Confession may well be amongst the sweetest, the most comforting, and the most decisive moments of life.**

Blessed Paul VI

**1** Give the children a
moment to explore
the illustration.

**2** As they explore, tell the
children your favorite
part about receiving
Communion. You may
not realize it but many
of the children in your
class are unaware that
receiving Communion
for the first time is a big
moment in their lives.
Your excitement will go
a long way in helping
them to build anticipation
toward receiving this
amazing gift.

**Thoughts become
choices, choices
becomes actions,
actions become
habits, habits
become character,
and your character
is your destiny.**

Decision Point

# First Communion

Your journey with God is a great spiritual journey. Along the
way you will have many decisions to make. Some will be big and
some will be small. Every decision you make changes who you are
forever. This is just one of the many reasons that God wants to
help you become a fabulous decision maker.

You are preparing for your First Communion. Receiving Jesus in
the Eucharist is one of the greatest blessings of our lives. But Holy
Communion is not just a one time blessing. It is a lifelong blessing.
Receiving Jesus in the Eucharist each and every Sunday at Mass
will fill you with everything you need to live a fabulous life.

**My Notes:**

_____

_____

_____

_____

_____

_____

_____

2 minutes

**tip**

Remember, one of the most powerful tools you have to lead this group is your story. If you have a picture of yourself at First Communion or one of your children bring it and share. If you don't have one with you for this class, make it a point to bring it for the next time you meet.

**For whenever you eat this bread and drink this cup, you proclaim the Lord's death until he comes.**

Corinthians 11:26

# READ AND EXPLORE

## Step-by-Step

**1** Tell the children you are going to read the last paragraph out loud because it contains a special reminder of how amazing God is.

**2** Read the last paragraph out loud.

Jesus gives himself to you in the Eucharist. He gives you his encouragement so that you can persevere in times of difficulty. And he gives you his wisdom so you can become a great decision maker.

After your First Communion you will be able to receive Jesus in the Eucharist every Sunday for the rest of your life. In the Eucharist, Jesus wants to encourage you. He wants to help you persevere in times of difficulty, he wants to give you the wisdom you need to become a great decision maker, and he wants to teach you how to be a good friend to others.

**My Notes:**

**There is no better way to receive God's grace than through the Eucharist.**

Decision Point

One of the promises Jesus made to the disciples before he ascended into heaven was that he would always be with us. Jesus keeps this promise in the Eucharist. We go to church on Sunday to be with Jesus. In fact, anytime you are confused or upset or have some great news to share, it's great to stop by church and sit with Jesus for a few minutes. He waits for us in the tabernacle. It is a great blessing that Jesus will always be with us in the Eucharist.

**2 minutes**

God doesn't call us to church on Sunday because he has some egotistical need for us all to fall down and worship him at ten o'clock each Sunday morning. It isn't designed to help him; it's designed to help us. The Mass is filled with riches. It is an unfathomable gift. Encourage your students to embrace the gift, even now, as they prepare for their First Communion.

**If angels could be jealous of men, they would be so for one reason: Holy Communion.**

St. Maximilian Kolbe

15

## Step-by-Step

**1** Ask the children: "What would the world be like if Mary said no to the mission God created her for?"

Possible answers:

- WE WOULDN'T HAVE JESUS.
- NO ONE WOULD BE SAVED.
- MARY WOULD HAVE BEEN REALLY UNHAPPY.

**You have a choice. Are you a child of God or a slave to the world?**

Decision Point

# Confirmation

God wants a dynamic collaboration with you. He doesn't just want to wave his hand and have everything happen exactly as he wants it to. God loves friendship and he wants to be your friend.

Before Jesus came to earth, an angel appeared to Mary and asked her if she would be willing to be mother to the Savior of the world. Mary said, "Yes!"

God didn't need Mary. He could have saved the world all by himself. But God didn't want it that way. God wanted a dynamic friendship with Mary.

God wants a dynamic friendship with you too.

But imagine what the world would be like if Mary didn't say yes? What would have happened if she said no to the mission God created her for?

**My Notes:**

_____

_____

_____

_____

_____

_____

_____

_____

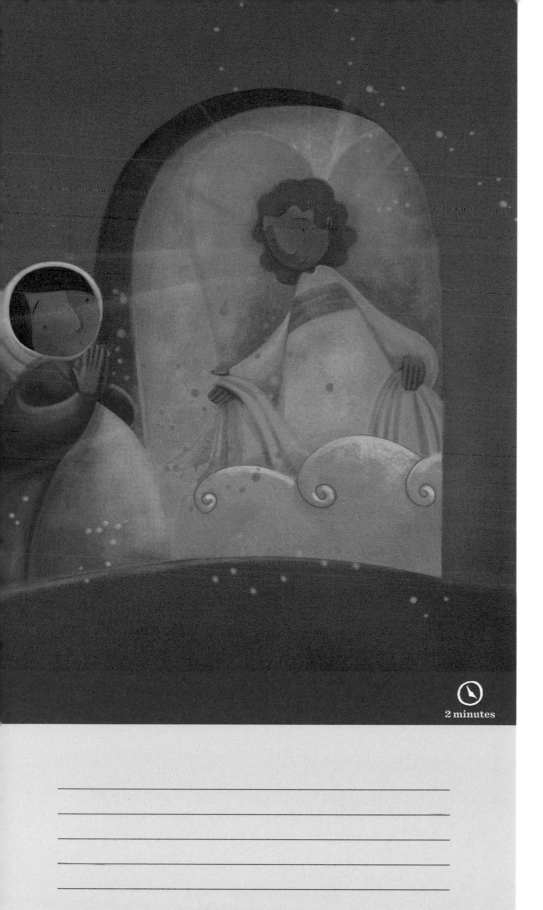

2 minutes

**tip**

If time allows, take a moment and make the connection between saying yes to God and your leading this class. Tell them, that of all the places in the world you could be, you have accepted God's invitation to be right here right now with them. Tell them there is no place you would rather be and no group of children you would rather be with. Children are always more likely to trust and respect a leader who values them. Be that leader.

**Through Mary we learn to surrender to God's will in all things. From Mary we learn to trust even when all hope seems gone. From Mary we learn to love Christ her son and the Son of God!**

St. John Paul II

# READ AND EXPLORE

## Step-by-Step

**1** Give the children the opportunity to explore the illustration of Noah's Ark. Don't rush. Allow time for questions. Ask them to share with you their favorite part. Share your favorite part of the illustration too.

**2** Invite a child to read the first paragraph out loud to the class.

**And Noah did all that the Lord had commanded him.**

Genesis 7:5

18

God has created you for a special mission. There is a whole lot of need in the world. People are hungry and lonely and sick and scared. Your mission is to respond to some of that need. Your mission is going to ease the suffering of many. But, just like Mary, you have to choose whether or not you accept God's mission for your life.

Some people wonder why the world got to be such a mess. They wonder why is there so much pain and suffering in the world. The reason is simple: the world is a mess because lots of people said no to God and rejected their mission. When people say no to God and yes to selfishness, the world becomes a mess.

Just like Mary and the saints, you were made for mission. Say yes to God.

When you are a little older, you will receive the Sacrament of Confirmation. This is another amazing Sacrament. Through the Sacrament of Confirmation God will fill you with the Holy Spirit so that you can discover and fulfill the mission God has entrusted to you.

**My Notes:**

_____

_____

_____

_____

_____

_____

_____

_____

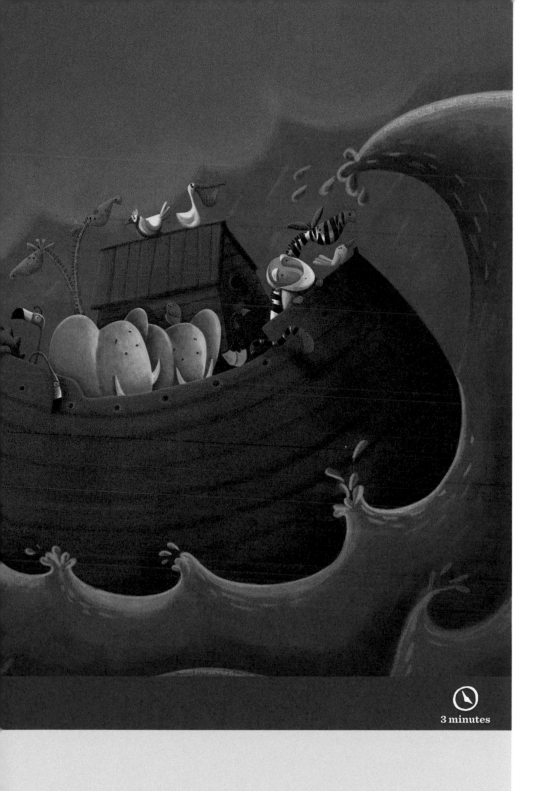

3 minutes

**tip**

Why is an illustration of Noah's ark placed within the context of Confirmation? God invited Noah to participate in his mission in small ways his whole life. When God saw that Noah was faithful in the small missions, God gave him something bigger to do. God kept asking Noah to do bigger things, and Noah kept saying yes. God prepared Noah for his mission his entire life. In the same way, God is preparing each child for his or her mission in life. Confirmation will be an important moment in their journey, but remind them that even now God is preparing them for their special mission in life by giving them little opportunities to say yes to him throughout the day.

**Love and do what you will. If you keep silence, do it out of love. If you cry out, do it out of love. If you refrain from punishing, do it out of love.**

St. Augustine of Hippo

19

## READ AND EXPLORE

### Step-by-Step

**1** Have a child read aloud the last paragraph.

**2** Take a break! Turn some music on, invite the children to stand up. Lead them in a stretch and a few dance moves to shake off any restlessness. Encourage them to reach for the sky, roll their shoulders forward and backward, and do some jumping jacks in place. Let them know they have your permission to have some fun! If possible, play the song "Beautiful Day" from *Blessed: A Collection of Songs for the Young at Heart.*

**Blessed is the couple who understands their marriage as a pathway to heaven.**

Allen Hunt

# Marriage

God loves relationships, and he has a great desire for you to have fabulous relationships. One of the relationships he may choose to bless you with is marriage.

In the Sacrament of Marriage, God brings a man and a woman together to cherish each other, to love one another, and to help each other become the-best-version-of-themselves, grow in virtue, and live a holy life together.

**My Notes:**

_____

_____

_____

_____

_____

_____

_____

_____

If you go to a wedding, you might hear a passage read from St. Paul about love. His words have inspired every generation to love as God loves:

**Love is patient and kind; love is not jealous or boastful; it is not arrogant or rude. Love does not insist on its own way; it is not irritable or resentful; it does not rejoice at wrong, but rejoices in the right. Love bears all things, believes all things, hopes all things, endures all things."**

1 Corinthians 13:4–7

🕐 **2 minutes**

**tip**

In John 10:10, Jesus says: "I came that they may have life and have it to the fullest." Jesus reminds us that life is meant to be enjoyed. Because the task of passing the faith along to the next generation is so important, we can sometimes forget that it's supposed to be enjoyable for the children. So, from time to time, at the appropriate moments, grant the children the permission to laugh and be silly. If you are comfortable, join them in their fun!

**Man is created in the image and likeness of God who is himself love. Since God created him man and woman, their mutual love becomes an image of the absolute and unfailing love with which God loves man.**

CCC, 1604

21

**Step-by-Step**

1. Give the children time to explore the illustration.

2. Ask the children: "Why did Jesus choose to wash the feet of his disciples?"

   • JESUS WANTED TO TEACH US THAT EVERYONE IS CALLED TO SERVE.

**Within you there is a hidden potential to be great. Everybody can be great because everybody can serve.**

Mustard Seeds

## Holy Orders

Each Sunday the priest celebrates Mass. He blesses you, leads you in prayer, teaches you, sings with you, and nourishes your soul with the Body and Blood of Jesus.

But have you ever wondered what your priest does during the week?

Throughout the week, your priest visits the sick, prays for you and everyone in your parish, says Mass each day, buries the dead, spends time with the lonely, and encourages those in despair. But he does lots of ordinary things too, like exercise and eat, read and visit with family and friends.

**My Notes:**

_____

_____

_____

_____

_____

_____

_____

Jesus laid his life down for us. He laid his life down for us on the cross, and he calls us all to lay down our lives for each other. A priest lays down his life to love God and serve God's people. It is the mission of the priest to love God by serving his people.

Since the time of Jesus, God has been choosing men to serve his people. In the Sacrament of Holy Orders, the Church ordains these men as deacons, priests, and bishops.

On the night before he died on the cross, Jesus washed the feet of his disciples. In Jesus' time only servants and slaves washed the feet of those in power. But Jesus was different. By example, Jesus showed that everyone is called to serve.

2 minutes

**tip**
Repetition is critical to retaining information. In this session, there is a lot for the children to process. It is only natural for their minds to try and prioritize the information they receive. By using repetition, you can help them focus in on the most important details and help ensure that each child is able to get the most out of every page.

**The Son of Man did not come to be served but to serve and to give his life as a ransom for many.**

Matthew 20:28

**Step-by-Step**

**1** Have a different child read a paragraph out loud.

**2** Take the time to say thank you to each child for reading and compliment them on a job well done. For example: "Cindy, you read that section so well. I really like the way you use your voice to make it sound like someone is talking."

**You are surrounded by miracles. And part of Jesus' invitation is for you to bring the miracle of his love to others.**

Rediscover Jesus

## Anointing of the Sick

Every day miracles are dancing all around us. We read in the Gospels of Matthew, Mark, Luke, and John about Jesus' miracles: turning water into wine; healing the sick; making the blind see, the deaf hear, and the lame walk; casting out demons; feeding thousands; raising people from the dead; calming storms; and walking on water.

One day, four men carried their paralyzed friend on a mat to see Jesus. But when they arrived at the house where Jesus was teaching, they couldn't get inside. There were too many people.

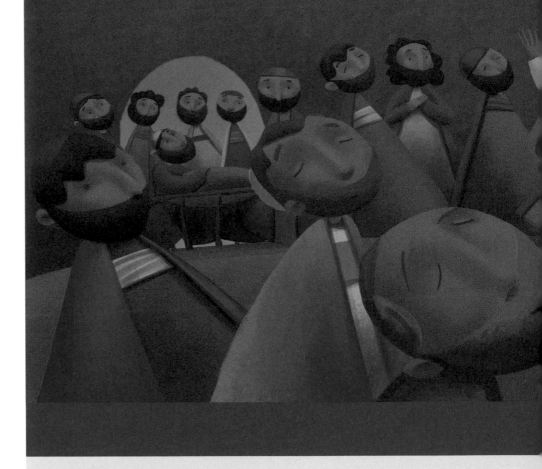

**My Notes:**
_____
_____
_____
_____
_____
_____
_____

The four men wanted so badly to help their friend that they went up on the roof and lowered him into the house before Jesus. Seeing the faith of these men, Jesus healed the paralyzed man, who immediately stood up and walked away.

You are on a great journey with God. If along the way you get sick and need God's healing for body, mind, or spirit, you will be blessed with the Anointing of the Sick.

2 minutes

**tip**
Some children will not want to read to the group. Anything from difficulty in reading to shyness may come into play. For that reason, be ready to jump in and read as needed.

He will provide the way and the means, such as you could never have imagined. Leave it all to him, let go of yourself, lose yourself on the cross, and you will find yourself entirely.

St. Catherine of Siena

## READ AND EXPLORE

### Step-by-Step

**1** Introduce the next passage by saying: "I'm going to read about healing now. Listen with your best ears."

**2** Read the passage out loud.

**3** Ask the children: "Which of these great Catholic Moments are you most looking forward to receiving?"

- FIRST COMMUNION
- CONFIRMATION
- MARRIAGE
- HOLY ORDERS
- ANOINTING OF THE SICK

**God is willing to do all the heavy lifting. He yearns for our cooperation, but he will not go where he is not invited.**

Rediscover Catholicism

Throughout your life, you will experience these great Catholic Moments we call Sacraments. Each of them is a blessing and they are all connected. These great Moments are designed by God to help you live a good life here on earth and prepare you to be blissfully happy with God forever in heaven.

You are blessed!

**My Notes:**

_____

_____

_____

_____

_____

_____

_____

**2 minutes**

**tip**

Learn to give the one gift you were born to give—yourself. There is no faster way to happen upon the purpose of your life than to embrace life's daily opportunities to serve those around you. In a special way, embrace every opportunity you have to serve the children before you. In every moment that you are with them, choose to be your best self. Allow yourself to be challenged to become the person God created you to be. Help the children to do the same. Here is one way to get started: As the students answer your question about which of the above they are looking most forward to receiving, be ready with some positive feedback. For example, you can say things like: "That's a good answer. What makes that one the one you are looking most forward to?"

**People who suffer have something to offer God. When they succeed in enduring their suffering, that is a daily miracle.**

St. Andre Bessette

## WATCH AND DISCUSS

### Step-by-Step

**1** Introduce Episode 3 by saying: "In this episode, Sarah plays fetch with Hemingway."

**2** Watch Episode 3.

**Life is wonderful but brief. Each day is filled with unimaginable potential. The life God invites us to allows us to live each moment consciously and with vibrant enthusiasm.**

Rediscover Catholicism

## God Loves to Celebrate

We celebrate a lot as Catholics. We celebrate Easter and Christmas, we celebrate feast days and birthdays, we celebrate God, and we celebrate each other. Have you ever wondered why we celebrate so much as Catholics? The reason is because God loves to celebrate.

### Favorite Days

Every day is special in its own way because life is special. Every day of life should be treasured. Life is precious. Life is sacred. Life is special.

**My Notes:**

_____

_____

_____

_____

_____

_____

_____

_____

Still, we all have favorites—favorite colors, favorite songs, and favorite foods. Do you have favorite days?

Some of my favorite days each year are Christmas, Easter, my birthday, and the feast days of my favorite saints. What are your three favorite days each year?

## Your Special Day

God gives everyone a special day each year. We call this your birthday. What do you like to do on your birthday? What is your favorite birthday memory?

**4 minutes**

### tip

Why do Catholics celebrate the lives of the saints? Many reasons. But the most important reason for you and the children right now is that they remind us of the personal invitation to become holy. The goal of the Christian life is to live a holy life. Those who have attained this goal we call saints. They found their essential purpose, they pursued their essential purpose, and they celebrated their essential purpose. The saints quietly chiseled away at the defects and weaknesses in their character. They became the-best-version-of-themselves. They have brought the Gospel to life, animating it with their own thoughts, words, and actions. And we celebrate them because they remind us that we can do the same.

**I give praise to you, Father, Lord of Heaven and earth, for although you have hidden these things from the wise and the learned you have revealed them to little ones.**

Matthew 11:25

29

## READ AND EXPLORE

### Step-by-Step

**1** Before reading the story of Zacchaeus, set the following expectation: "Listen for what happens to Zacchaeus after the first time he meets Jesus."

**2** Read the story of the first time Zacchaeus meets Jesus on page 30.

**Isn't it time you gave yourself to God completely, once and for all?**

Mustard Seeds

## The First Time

Firsts matter. The first time you get to do anything is important. You never get that first time again.

Throughout the Gospels we often hear fabulous stories about the first time people met Jesus. One of the great examples of this is the story of Zacchaeus, a tax collector who was known for being a dishonest man.

One day when Jesus was walking, a huge crowd followed him, making it very difficult for anyone to see him. Zacchaeus wanted to see Jesus so badly that he climbed a tree just to catch a glimpse of him!

That first meeting with Jesus completely changed Zacchaeus' life. He renounced his dishonest ways and did his best to make up for all he had done wrong.

**My Notes:**

_____

_____

_____

_____

_____

_____

_____

_____

**tip**

Your page numbers match the page numbers in the student workbook. So the story of Zacchaeus appears on pages 30 and 31 in both this book and the students'.

Firsts can be very special.

As we prepare for your First Communion, let's remember that you will never have this first again.

Every Sunday when you go to Mass you will be blessed to receive Jesus in the Eucharist. But there is something very special about the first time. So it is important for you to pay attention to everything that your parents and teachers are sharing with you about this very special event in your life.

You will never have this first again. Cherish it.

**2 minutes**

_____

_____

_____

_____

_____

_____

_____

**Never worry about numbers. Help one person at a time, and always start with the person nearest you.**

St. Teresa of Calcutta

## READ AND EXPLORE

### Step-by-Step

**1** Ask the children: "Who is your favorite saint?" and "Why does this saint inspire you?"

**For two thousand years, the champions of Christianity, the men and women we call saints, have been going into the classroom of silence, taking a humble and honest look at themselves, and assessing their own strengths and weaknesses. Then, armed with this knowledge, they have bravely set forth to transform their weaknesses into strengths, their vices into virtues.**

Rediscover Catholicism

## Feast Days

Catholics love to celebrate. So we have a whole year of celebrations planned. The high points of the Church's year are Christmas and Easter. But we also celebrate the great spiritual champions in our Catholic family. We call these men, women, and children saints!

Who is your favorite saint? When is his or her feast day? Why does this saint inspire you?

**My Notes:**

_____

_____

_____

_____

_____

_____

_____

2 minutes

**Let us never forget that if we wish to die like the saints we must live like them.**

St. Theodore Guerin

33

## READ AND EXPLORE

### Step-by-Step

**1** Take another stretch break! Invite the children to stand up. Lead them in a series of stretches and dance moves to shake off any restlessness. Encourage them to reach for the sky, roll their shoulders forward and backward, and do some jumping jacks in place. If possible, play music, like "Gratitude" from *Blessed: A Collection of Songs for the Young at Heart.* Let them know they have your permission to have some fun!

**Time is a precious gift. It is so precious that God dispenses it to you one second at a time. Don't waste time.**

Mustard Seeds

## God's Favorite Day

God loves spending time with us. He loves it when we take a few minutes each day to talk to him. He loves it when we come to visit him at church on Sunday. He loves spending time with you. God smiles when he sees you at Mass on Sunday.

Sunday is God's favorite day.

**My Notes:**

_____

_____

_____

_____

_____

_____

_____

_____

1 minutes

---

**tip**

When managing a classroom, one of the most important things you can do to help foster good behavior in the classroom is to develop a routine. Why? Because routines help children practice self-control, they reduce the opportunities for power struggles, and they allow the children to relax in a new environment. Below is a list of potential routines you can establish in the classroom. Some of these routines will work for your classroom and some won't. That's ok. The point is, the children's First Communion experience will be significantly enhanced with established routines.

- ENTERING AND EXITING THE CLASSROOM QUIETLY IN SINGLE FILE

- ASSIGNED SEATING

- A SIGNAL THAT INDICATES A TIME FOR THE CHILDREN TO QUIET DOWN AND FOCUS THEIR ATTENTION ON YOU

- WHENEVER A CHILD FINISHES AN ACTIVITY EARLY, THEY ARE ENCOURAGED TO EXPLORE THE REST OF THEIR WORKBOOK

- TURNING THE LIGHTS OFF BEFORE PLAYING AN EPISODE OF *BLESSED*

## WATCH AND DISCUSS

### Step-by-Step

**1** Introduce Episode 4 by saying: "In this episode, Ben, Max, and Elijah have a special surprise for a sleeping Tiny. Keep it to yourself when you realize what it is. We can discuss it afterward."

**2** Watch Episode 4.

**How many Sundays do you have left? Don't waste a single one.**

Decision Point

## What Makes Sunday Special?

Sunday is a special day.

Most people only get to enjoy about four thousand Sundays in their lives. Now, that may seem like a lot, but they go quickly. You have probably already experienced about 420 Sundays. So don't waste a single one. Make every Sunday a special day.

**My Notes:**

_____

_____

_____

_____

_____

_____

_____

_____

What are three ways you make Sunday a special day?
Go to church. Spend time with your family. Rest.

There are lots of special days, but most of them happen just once a year, and some of them only happen once in your lifetime. One of the beautiful things about Sunday is it happens every week.

Sunday is the Sabbath. The Sabbath is a special day of rest and worship.

We all need to take a break from time to time to rest. Each night we rest by sleeping. And once a week, God wants us to take a special rest so that we can be filled with joy and share that joy with everyone who comes into our lives.

The first story in the Bible is about God creating the world. He finished creating on the sixth day, and the Bible tells us that he rested on the seventh day. That's why we rest on Sunday. Rest is holy.

7 minutes

**tip**

From the beginning God set aside the Sabbath to be holy. If time allows, refer to Exodus 20:11: "For in six days the Lord made the heavens and the earth, the sea, and all that is in them, but he rested on the seventh day. Therefore the Lord blessed the Sabbath day and made it holy."

**Remember the Sabbath day by keeping it holy.**

Exodus 20:8

37

## READ AND EXPLORE

### Step-by-Step

**1** Have six volunteers read aloud six ways we can take care of ourselves.

**2** Ask the children: "What are you most grateful for today?"

**God loves a cheerful giver but he also loves those who are able to receive graciously and thankfully.**

Mustard Seeds

God loves you so much that he wants you to take good care of yourself.

We take care of ourselves by:

- Eating well
- Drinking plenty of water
- Exercising regularly
- Praying each day
- Getting enough sleep
- Resting on Sundays

**My Notes:**

_____

_____

_____

_____

_____

_____

_____

_____

Sunday is also a day of worship. We go to Mass to worship God. There are many ways to worship God, but one way we can do this every day is by thanking him for the many ways he has blessed us.

Have you counted your blessings today? What are you most grateful for today?

One of the things that make Sunday a special day is that we go to church. We praise and thank God by going to Mass each Sunday. What is the name of the church you go to for Mass on Sundays?

2 minutes

_____

_____

_____

_____

_____

_____

_____

**tip**

From time to time the material within this book should challenge you as a leader just as much as it challenges the children. This should be one of those moments. How many Sundays do you have left? When was the last time the Sabbath was really the Sabbath for you? Is Sunday a special day in your house? Spend some time self-reflecting on the importance you place on Sunday.

**Come to me, all you who are weary and burdened, and I will give you rest. Take my yoke upon you and learn from me, for I am gentle and humble in heart, and you will find rest for your souls.**

Matthew 11:28–30

## WATCH AND DISCUSS

### Step-by-Step

**1** Introduce Episode 5 by saying: "Have you ever wondered how God created the world? Well, let's find out together!"

**2** Watch Episode 5.

> **God's plea to humanity has always been a call to go within and discover the truth about ourselves, which is that we have been created in the image and likeness of God.**
>
> Mustard Seeds

# From the Bible: Creation

On the first day God created day and night, light and time.

On the second day God created the sky.

On the third day God created the earth, the seas, plants, and trees.

On the fourth day God created the sun, the moon, and the stars.

On the fifth day God created birds and fish.

On the sixth day God created cattle, insects, wild animals, and human beings.

And God didn't just create us; he created us in his image.

What does it mean that we are created in the image of God? It means God made us to resemble him. We can reason, we can dream, we know right from wrong, we are capable of holiness, and we thrive on healthy friendships.

**My Notes:**

_____

_____

_____

_____

_____

_____

_____

_____

To be made in the image of God is a great blessing, and blessings come with responsibility. God made humanity responsible stewards of all creation. He gave us the mind and the morality necessary to take care of all of creation.

When God had finished the work of creation, "he saw everything he had made, and indeed, it was very good" (Genesis 1:31).

God said—It is good! God blessed creation.

On the seventh day God rested. We call this the Sabbath, which means a day of rest and prayer.

5 minutes

_____

_____

_____

_____

_____

_____

_____

**tip**

The fifth episode in every session of this workbook is a story from the Bible. Why? 50 years of research shows that children thrive on routine. Our own research at Dynamic Catholic shows that making strong connections between the stories in the Bible and every day life is critical if we want Catholics to become lifelong readers of the Scriptures. Nothing about *Blessed* is random or accidental. Every place of this program is designed to drive desired outcomes. Take your time with these Bible passages. Read them slowly as if nobody has ever heard them before. One of the ways we respect the Word of God is simply in the way we read it. Remind the students that the Bible is a great way to learn valuable life lessons and grow closer to God. Share with the class that you wish you had immersed yourself in the wisdom of the Bible much earlier in your life or how much you enjoy spending time reading the Bible.

# READ AND EXPLORE

### Step-by-Step

**1** Ask the children: "What is one reason we go to Church on Sunday?"

- TO SAY THANK YOU TO GOD FOR ALL THE WAYS HE HAS BLESSED US THIS WEEK!

Sunday is a day of rest. God blessed rest by resting himself. By blessing rest he teaches us that rest is holy.

Sunday is also a day of gratitude.

One Sunday on the way to church, Max asked his dad, "Why do we go to church every Sunday?" His dad smiled and replied, "Lots of reasons. But one very important reason is to say thank you to God for all the ways he has blessed us this week."

**Ask the Holy Spirit to guide you and counsel you— and you will find yourself making better choices.**

Decision Point

**My Notes:**

_____

_____

_____

_____

_____

_____

_____

_____

_____

Every blessing comes from God!

Did you ever give someone a gift and he wasn't grateful? Perhaps he didn't say thank you, or maybe he tossed the gift aside as if it were a piece of junk. How did that make you feel?

God has blessed us with so many gifts. Going to Mass on Sunday is a great way to show God that we are grateful.

**3 minutes**

**tip**

Share with the children a time where you gave a gift to someone who didn't appreciate the gift. Share with them how that made you feel. When you're done, make the connection between how you felt and how God must feel when we don't make it to Church on Sunday.

**And let us consider how we may spur one another on toward love and good deeds.**

Hebrews 10:24

43

**Step-by-Step**

**1** Introduce Episode 6 by saying: "Have you ever wanted to hear the voice of God in your life? If so, show me thumbs up. If not, show me thumbs down. I am a thumbs up person! In this next episode, Ben and Sarah show us how to hear the voice of God in our lives!"

**2** Watch Episode 6.

We would do well to learn to listen to the deepest desires of our hearts, and we should follow them wherever they lead us regardless of the cost or sacrifice involved.

The Rhythm of Life

# Listening to God at Mass

Have you ever wondered, "What is God really like?" It's a great question. We know many things about God and still he is a beautiful mystery because we do not know everything about him.

We know that God is love. We know God keeps his promises. We know that God cares about every single person. We know that God knows everything. We know that God is holy. We know that God is all-powerful. We know God has a plan. And we know that God is unchanging.

In the Bible we read about God speaking to Adam and Eve, Noah, Abraham, Moses, Isaac, Jacob, Rebekah, Mary, and many others.

Remember the last thing we said we know about God? God is unchanging.

And just as he spoke to people in ancient times, he speaks to people in every time, and he speaks to you and me today. He speaks to us through the Scriptures. He speaks to us through other people. He speaks to us through the Church. And he speaks to us in our hearts.

At Mass on Sunday God wants to speak to you. I like to bring a little journal with me to Mass to jot down the things he says to me in my heart.

**My Notes:**

_____

_____

_____

_____

_____

_____

_____

I ask him at the beginning of Mass: "God, please show me one way in this Mass I can become a-better-version-of-myself this week." Then I listen to the readings, the prayers, the music, the homily, and the quiet of my heart, and write down the one thing that I sense God is saying to me.

Every Sunday at Mass, write the one thing God says to you in your Mass Journal. You will be amazed how God encourages you and challenges you to become the-best-version-of-yourself, grow in virtue, and live a holy life.

Every day is a new day in your journey with God—and every day God has a message he is trying to share with you.

5 minutes

**tip**

Later on, there will be a more extensive discussion around the Mass Journal. If you've never used one, now's the time to try it. How much more impactful will the lesson be if you brought your own Mass Journal into class to show the children? You would be able to share with them how God is speaking to you! See page 62 for more about the Mass Journal.

_____
_____
_____
_____
_____
_____
_____
_____

**Of all human activities, man's listening to God is the supreme act of his reasoning and will.**

Blessed Paul VI

## SHOW WHAT YOU KNOW

### Step-by-Step

**1** Have your children complete the activity page by themselves, with a partner, or as a group.

**2** After 3 minutes ask the class: "Are there any questions you are struggling with?"

**3** Briefly explain the answer to each question they have by referring back to the specific page in the workbook.

**Your weaknesses are the key to the unimaginable bigger future that God has envisioned for you.**

Rediscover Catholicism

## Show What You Know

### True or False

1. __T__ You are on a journey toward your First Communion. (p 2)

2. __T__ You are blessed. (p 3)

3. __F__ God never likes to celebrate. (p 28)

4. __T__ You will only have one First Communion in your life. (p 31)

5. __T__ Sunday is a day for gratitude. (p 42)

### Fill in the blank

1. You are on a great _____journey_____ with God. (p 25)

2. One of the greatest blessings you will ever receive in your life is the _____Eucharist_____. (p 2)

3. God is _____inviting_____ you to a great banquet. (p 2)

4. One way you can worship God every day is by counting your _____blessings_____. (p 39)

5. After God finished the work of creation, he said that everything was _____good_____, even insects! (p 41)

**My Notes:**

_____

_____

_____

_____

_____

_____

_____

_____

_____

6. God created us in _____**his**_____ image and likeness. (p 40)

7. Sunday is a special day for _____**rest**_____
   and _____**worship**_____ . (p 37, 39)

8. We _____**thank**_____ and _____**praise**_____ God by
   going to Mass each Sunday. (p 39)

9. Just as he did in ancient times, God _____**speaks**_____ to
   you and me. (p 44)

10. Going to Mass on Sunday is a great way to show God we are
    _____**grateful**_____ . (p 43)

**Word Bank**

| | | | | | | | |
|---|---|---|---|---|---|---|---|
| PRAISE | SPEAKS | JOURNEY | GOOD | THANK | INVITING | REST | HIS |
| | GRATEFUL | EUCHARIST | WORSHIP | BLESSINGS | | | |

🕐 **1 minutes**

**tip**

This is a long session and we have only alotted one minute to complete this activity. This is not enough time. Unless you are ahead of schedule, ask the children to complete the exercise for homework. Check to see if they finished the activity at the start of the next session.

**O my God, let me remember with gratitude and confess you your mercies toward me.**

St. Augustine of Hippo

# JOURNAL WITH JESUS

### Step-by-Step

**1** Invite your children to write a letter to Jesus.

**2** Help them brainstorm a few things they might want to say. Tell them not to worry about the spelling, but to focus on what they want to say.

**3** Ask the children to remain silent during their journaling time.

**4** You may wish to play some quiet, reflective music to help create the right mood in the classroom and to encourage the students to remain quiet and focused on journaling with Jesus.

**The Gospel is alive and active. It has the power to transform our lives, our communities, our nations, and even the whole world.**

Rediscover Catholicism

**My Notes:**

_____
_____
_____
_____
_____
_____
_____

## Journal with Jesus

Dear Jesus,

Sundays are special because . . .

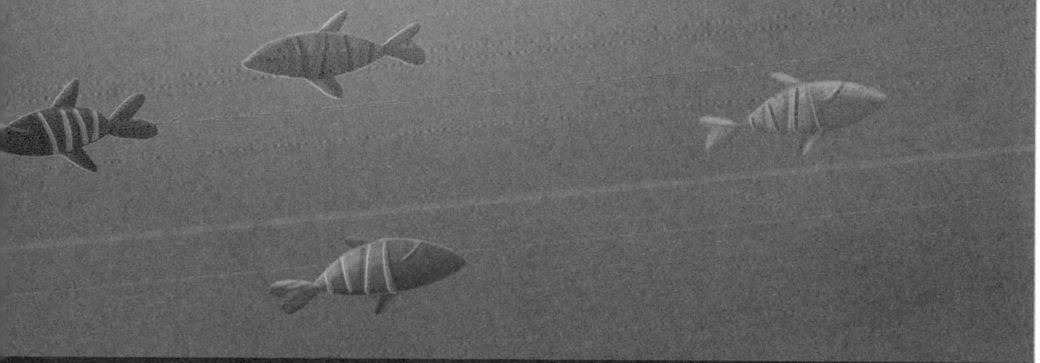

3 minutes

### tip

Some of the children will write more than others. That's ok. However, the children who finish early will be tempted to talk and distract those who are still working. To help keep everyone focused, walk around the class as they write and peek over their shoulders. This will encourage them to write more and let them know that you are taking this exercise seriously.

**The more we let God take us over, the more truly ourselves we become—because he made us. He invented us . . . it is when I turn to Christ, when I give myself to his personality, that I first begin to have a real personality of my own.**

C.S. Lewis

# CLOSING PRAYER

## Step-by-Step

**1** Introduce Episode 7 by saying: "It's time for the closing prayer. Let's quiet down and get ready to pray with Sarah."

**2** Watch Episode 7.

**3** Ask your children: "What are some of the most important things you learned in this session?"

- THE EUCHARIST IS ONE OF THE GREATEST BLESSINGS IN LIFE.
- SUNDAY IS GOD'S FAVORITE DAY.
- GOD LOVES SPENDING TIME WITH ME, AND HE LOVES SEEING ME AT MASS ON SUNDAY.
- GOING TO MASS ON SUNDAY IS A GREAT WAY TO SHOW GOD HOW GRATEFUL I AM.

## Closing Prayer

When Zechariah's son, John the Baptist, was born, he was overwhelmed with gratitude. After months of not being able to speak, Zechariah burst into a song of praise, thanking God for all the incredible gifts he had been given.

Zechariah reminds us of the importance of voicing our gratitude to God.

Jesus is with us always in the Eucharist. This is an incredible gift! To show God how grateful we are for the gift of Jesus, let's praise him using the words of Zechariah:

**My Notes:**

_____

_____

_____

_____

_____

_____

_____

_____

Blessed be the Lord,
The God of Israel;
He has come to his people and set them free.

He has raised up for us a mighty Savior,
Born of the house of his servant David.

Through his holy prophets he promised of old
That he would save us from our enemies,
From the hands of all who hate us.

He promised to show mercy to our fathers
And to remember his holy Covenant.

This was the oath he swore to our father Abraham:
To set us free from the hands of our enemies,
Free to worship him without fear,
Holy and righteous in his sight
All the days of our life.

From Luke 1:68–75

**3 minutes**

**tip**
Thank your children
for coming. Never stop
thanking them for coming.
Tell them you enjoyed your
time with them. Identify a
moment in the class that
you thought was particularly
powerful. Remind them you
are praying for them.

_____

_____

_____

_____

_____

_____

_____

**One must arrange
one's life so
that everything
praises God.**

St. John Paul II

51

# 2

# The Greatest Event on Earth

## QUICK SESSION OVERVIEW

Opening Prayer. . . . . . . . . . . . . . . . . . . . . . . . . . . . . . . . . . 4 min

Watch and Discuss; Read and Explore . . . . . . . . . . . . . .61 min

Show What You Know . . . . . . . . . . . . . . . . . . . . . . . . . . 10 min

Journal with Jesus. . . . . . . . . . . . . . . . . . . . . . . . . . . . . 10 min

Closing Prayer. . . . . . . . . . . . . . . . . . . . . . . . . . . . . . . . . 5 min

## OBJECTIVES

- **TO PROCLAIM** that the Mass is the most amazing event on earth.

- **TO EXPLAIN** that spending time with God fills us with grace so that we can live holy lives.

- **TO TEACH** that learning to listen to God's voice is one of life's greatest lessons.

# • Jesus wants you to succeed.
# • Gratitude is a powerful tool.

## WELCOME

Before you is a sacred opportunity to serve God's children. They are near and dear to his heart and deserve to know just how much he loves them.

By saying yes to this great opportunity, you have made a remarkable and highly commendable choice. **Thank you** for making it.

Make no mistake, the task before you is a big one. But don't let this worry you. After all, you are not alone. Jesus wants you to succeed.

In Matthew 19:14, Jesus says, "Let the little children come to me . . ."

Jesus wants your little children to come to him, and he assists those who work diligently toward that goal in powerful ways. So, as you prepare these children for their First Communion, remember God is with you, filling you with the grace you need to be your best.

The great evangelist and teacher St. Paul knew the challenges that face those who seek to share the Good News. The following is a part of his letter to the Colossians. May this prayer echo through the centuries and sink deep into your heart.

> *Let the peace of Christ rule your hearts, to which indeed you were called in the one body. Be thankful. Let the word of Christ dwell in you richly; teach and admonish one another in all wisdom; and with gratitude in your hearts sing psalms, hymns, and spiritual songs to God. And whatever you do, in word or deed, do everything in the name of the Lord Jesus, giving thanks to God the Father through him.*

Colossians 3:15-17

**Prayer Icon**

**Read and Explore**

**Watch and Discuss**

**Show What You Know**

**Journal with Jesus**

**Time Tracker**

# OPENING PRAYER

### Step-by-Step

**1** Gather students for prayer.

**2** Wait for them to be quiet. Don't rush this; reverence takes patience and practice. Before reading the prayer aloud, take a deep breath to allow an additional moment of silence. You never know what God might say to your students (or you!) when given the opportunity.

**Regardless of the best plan you can put together for yourself with the greatest of your imagination, God has something much greater planned. If only you will surrender.**

Mustard Seeds

**My Notes:**

_____

_____

_____

_____

_____

_____

_____

# 2

# The Greatest Event on Earth

God, our loving Father,
thank you for all the ways you bless me.
Help me to be aware that every person,
place, and adventure I experience is an
opportunity to love you more.
Fill me with a desire to change and to grow,
and give me the grace to become
the-best-version-of-myself in
every moment of every day.

Amen.

🕐
**4 minutes**

_____

_____

_____

_____

_____

_____

_____

## tip

Being specific lets your students know what is needed. Here are two examples of specific, direct instructions:

1. "We are not talking right now; we are praying."
2. "I am waiting on everyone to close their eyes to begin."

**Rejoice always, pray continually, give thanks in all circumstances; for this is God's will for you in Christ Jesus.**

1 Thessalonians 5:16–18

## WATCH AND DISCUSS

### Step-by-Step

**1** Introduce Episode 1 by saying: "In this episode, Hemingway helps Ben settle a disagreement between Jessica and Max. As you watch, be on the lookout for how many types of prayer there are. See how many you can count."

**2** Watch Episode 1.

**3** Ask: "How many types of prayer are there? What are the types of prayer?"

1. THANKSGIVING
2. PETITION AND INTERCESSION
3. PRAISE
4. ADORATION

If they need help finding the answer, point to the text in the workbook.

## Love desires what is good for the other person.

Decision Point

# The Ultimate Prayer

You are blessed. One of the greatest blessings God gives us as Catholics is the Mass.

There are many different types of prayer. There are prayers of thanksgiving, in which we thank God for all the ways he blesses us. There are prayers of petition or intercession, in which we ask God for some favor. There are prayers of praise, in which we praise God for being God. And there are prayers of adoration, in which we adore God.

**My Notes:**

_____

_____

_____

_____

_____

_____

_____

_____

One of the incredible things about the Mass is that it combines all these forms of prayer. This is just one of the many reasons why the Mass is the ultimate prayer. Another reason is because in it we present a perfect offering to God. Jesus, who died for us on the cross, is that perfect offering.

Each time you receive Jesus in Holy Communion, God will fill you up in a special way with his grace so that you can become the-best-version-of-yourself!

It is a great privilege to go to Mass each Sunday. The Mass is the ultimate prayer. It is the perfect way for us to gather together as a community of believers and praise God.

At Mass we remember Jesus' last meal, his death on the cross, and his Resurrection. We also get to receive him in the Eucharist. The Eucharist is a celebration of God's love for us and a reminder that God is always with us.

Your First Communion is going to be a very special day in your life.

**10 minutes**

_____
_____
_____
_____
_____
_____
_____
_____

**If we really understood the Mass, we would die of joy.**

St. John Vianney

## WATCH AND DISCUSS

### Step-by-Step

**1** Introduce Episode 2 by saying: "In this episode, Sarah and her dad take a trip to God's house."

**2** Watch Episode 2.

**3** Ask: "Where is God's house?"

- THE CHURCH!

Emphasize that your own parish is one of God's houses.

**Before we make a decision, particularly a large one, it is wise for each of us to take time in the classroom of silence to listen to the gentle voice within.**

The Rhythm of Life

## God's House

Where do we celebrate Mass? At God's house! That's right. The church is God's house. God is so brilliant that he knew in his almighty wisdom that it would be important for us to spend time with him at his house.

Why? Well, have you ever noticed that when you are around people who are good, kind, generous, and thoughtful, you get inspired to be good, kind, generous, and thoughtful too?

When we spend time with God he inspires us to be good— and not just good, but our best. God wants you to live the best life imaginable and he wants you to become the-best-version-of-yourself, grow in virtue, and live a holy life.

**My Notes:**

_____

_____

_____

_____

_____

_____

_____

_____

When we spend time with God, he fills us with his grace so that we can live holy lives. So each Sunday he invites us over to his house for a great celebration. We call that celebration the Mass. But God is always happy to see us. Sometimes it is nice just to stop by church in the middle of the week and sit in the pews and talk to God about whatever is happening in your life. He loves it when we talk to him about what is happening in our lives.

6 minutes

**tip**

Over and over throughout the Gospels we read about Jesus going to quiet places to pray. Why did Jesus withdraw so often to pray? He withdrew to pray so that he could stay focused on his mission and be reminded what really mattered. We all get confused about what really matters from time to time. Prayer helps us to keep things in perspective. Give prayer a central place in your teaching philosophy. Pray for the children and their families. Pray with the children. And ask the Holy Spirit to be with you in a powerful way throughout this process.

## But Jesus often withdrew to lonely places and prayed.

Luke 5:16

57

## WATCH AND DISCUSS

### Step-by-Step

**1** Introduce Episode 3 by saying: "In this episode, Tiny asks Sr. Rosa if he really has to go to Mass every Sunday. Let's see how she answers the question!"

**2** Watch Episode 3.

**3** Ask the children: "What is one reason why it is important to go to Mass each Sunday?"

- TO THANK GOD FOR ALL THE WAYS HE BLESSES US!

**The ability to delay gratification is intimately linked with success. You cannot succeed at anything unless you are willing and able to delay gratification.**

Resisting Happiness

## The Third Commandment

When Moses went to the top of Mount Sinai to speak with God, God didn't give him one hundred commandments or a thousand commandments. How many commandments did God give Moses to share with the people?

That's right. Just ten.

Do you remember what we said about the Ten Commandments when we were preparing for your First Reconciliation? Let's take another look.

> The Ten Commandments are a blessing from God given to his people. They help us become the-best-version-of-ourselves, grow in virtue, and live holy lives. They show us the best way to live.

And because there are so few, every single one is very important.

Do you remember what the third commandment is? That's right. "Remember to keep holy the Lord's Day."

**My Notes:**

_____

_____

_____

_____

_____

_____

_____

Sunday is the Lord's Day. It is the Sabbath. It is God's day. And this is really important to remember. How do we keep the Sabbath holy? By going to Mass.

Going to Mass is the most important thing on Sunday. God wants to see us and spend time with us. Even if we have a soccer game or a camping trip, God still expects us to plan a time to go to Mass.

He gives you life every moment of every day. He fills your life with fabulous opportunities. He blesses you in so many ways. And he asks that you visit him for one hour each week.

How many hours are there in a week? There are seven days in a week, and twenty-four hours in a day: 7 x 24 = 168. Out of 168 hours each week, God asks that you come to his house for one hour. Is that too much to ask?

We should be excited to get there each Sunday to thank God for all the ways he has blessed us, to thank him for life, and just to spend time with him.

7 minutes

**tip**

Keep your sense of humor close by. Teaching the Catholic faith is a serious task; there's probably nothing more important. But it's also supposed to be fun. You never want to lose sight of the joy of being with young children. When a child does something humorous, share in his or her delight. While sarcasm is not recommended for this age group, laughter is!

**Taste and see how good the Lord is; blessed the man who takes refuge in him.**

Psalm 34:8

## WATCH AND DISCUSS

**Step-by-Step**

**1** Introduce Episode 4 by saying: "Do you think God still speaks to his people? Thumbs up if you think yes. Thumbs down if you think no. Let's watch and find out!"

**2** Watch Episode 4.

**3** Ask the children: "Last time you were at church, what did God say to you?" After such an important question, be sure to give the children a moment to think about it. Be ready to answer the question yourself as well.

**From time to time it is good for us all to learn to listen again. Listen to those you love. Listen to your soul. Listen to God.**

Resisting Happiness

# Listening to God

When you get to church each Sunday it is good to take a few minutes to get quiet before Mass begins. This helps us to hear what God wants to say to us.

God speaks to us in so many ways.

God speaks to us through the Bible. He speaks to us through the Church. He speaks to us in our hearts. He speaks to us through other people and through situations. And he speaks to our hearts in a special way at Mass.

Learning to listen to God's voice is one of the most important lessons we can learn in life. But learning to hear his voice clearly takes a lot of practice. One great way to practice is at Mass on Sunday. In some ways, we come to Mass on Sunday to get our instructions for the week from God.

**My Notes:**

_____

_____

_____

_____

_____

_____

_____

_____

You probably won't hear an actual voice when God speaks to you. He might speak to you through one of the readings, or through the music or homily, or he may just speak to you in the quiet of your heart.

God might say, "I want you to practice being more patient with your little brother this week." He might say, "I want you to listen to your parents and do what they ask you to do without hesitation." Or he might say, "I want you to enjoy nature while you are on your vacation this week."

God has a special message for us every week. That's why it's important to go to Mass every Sunday. Without God's instructions and directions, we get lost.

Every Sunday at church God has something he wants to tell you. It's unique every week. That's why he invites you to come to Mass every Sunday, so you can hear the special thing he wants to say to you.

Last time you were at church, what did God say to you? Do you remember? Were you listening?

**10 minutes**

**tip**

I want to encourage you to repeat this question, "Last time you were at church, what did God say to you?" Too often we see repetition as a bad thing, but it is one of the great tools at every teacher's disposal. If you ask the children consistently what God is saying to them, it will make its way into their psyche. Slowly but surely, they will begin to actively listen for what God has to say.

**As much as possible, be alone with God so that you can listen to him. He will speak in the silence of your heart.**

St. Teresa of Calcutta

## READ AND EXPLORE

### Step-by-Step

**1** Invite the children to explore the illustration.

**2** Activity: SIMON SAYS
To play, perform a quick movement, like touching your nose, and tell the children to do the same. The children should touch their noses only if you say, "Simon says," first. If any children touch their noses without your saying, "Simon says," they are out and should sit down. Work fast to make it more difficult and to add humor. The sillier the movement, the more fun the group will have. Play until all the children are sitting or two minutes have passed.

**Christianity is inconvenient. But it will bring you a joy that you have not even imagined yet.**

Decision Point

## Your Mass Journal

Do you ever feel like God is trying to tell you something? God is always trying to speak to us, but learning to listen to God in the many ways he speaks to us takes time and practice.

When God spoke to Jonah, he told Jonah about a very special mission he had planned for him. Well, Jonah didn't like what God was asking him to do, so instead of listening to God, Jonah tried to run away.

But God didn't give up on Jonah. Instead, God sent a giant whale to swallow Jonah whole! For three days and three nights Jonah lived in the belly of the whale. Once Jonah finally started listening to God, God rescued Jonah from the whale and sent him off to fulfill his mission.

**My Notes:**

_____

_____

_____

_____

_____

_____

_____

_____

5 minutes

**tip**

Listening skills are necessary for learning and building relationships. This is especially true when it comes to learning to listen to God! Explain to the candidates that one of the practical life skills they are developing is the ability to really listen to God. "Simon Says" is a great way to help the children learn the importance of listening in a fun and entertaining way.

## The word of the Lord came to Jonah son of Amittai.

Jonah 1:1

## Step-by-Step

**1** Ask the children: "What is one of the reasons we go to Mass on Sunday?"

- TO LISTEN TO GOD'S VOICE

**2** If they have trouble answering the question, ask one of the children to read the last sentence of the last paragraph.

**Develop the ability to say everything without saying anything. Action is the loudest voice.**

Mustard Seeds

God has always spoken to his people. And he wants to speak to you too.

Next Sunday, take a little notebook to Mass with you. This will be your Mass Journal. Listen to the music, listen to the readings, listen to the prayers, listen to the homily, and listen to your heart. Before Mass begins, pray, "Dear God, please show me one way in this Mass that I can become a-better-version-of-myself this week."

Then listen, wait patiently, and when you sense the one thing that God is saying to you, write it down. Pray for the rest of the Mass about how you can live that one thing this week, and ask God to help you.

There are many wonderful reasons why we go to Mass on Sunday, and one of them is to listen to God's voice.

**My Notes:**

_____

_____

_____

_____

_____

_____

_____

_____

**5 minutes**

**tip**

What is your favorite way to listen to God's voice? Going to Sunday Mass, sitting quietly in Church, praying at home, reading Scripture, or some other way? Whatever it is, share it with the children.

**If we wish to make any progress in the service of God we must begin every day of our life with new eagerness.**

St. Charles Borromeo

65

## WATCH AND DISCUSS

### Step-by-Step

**1** Introduce Episode 5 by saying: "I hope you are as excited as I am to hear the story of the two disciples who meet Jesus on the road to Emmaus!"

**2** Watch Episode 5.

**It is through prayer, reflection, the Scriptures, the grace of the sacraments, the wisdom of the Church, and the guidance of the Holy Spirit that we discover and walk the path that God is calling us to walk.**

Rediscover Catholicism

## From the Bible: The Road to Emmaus

A few days after Jesus rose from the dead, two of his disciples were walking from Jerusalem to a village called Emmaus. They were talking about Jesus and all the incredible things that had happened. While they were talking Jesus came up beside them, but their eyes were kept from recognizing him. He said to them, "What are you talking about?"

They stopped and looked at him. Then one of them said, "Are you the only person in Jerusalem who does not know the things that have taken place there the past few days?"

**My Notes:**

_____

_____

_____

_____

_____

_____

_____

"What things?" he asked them.

"The things about Jesus of Nazareth, a great and wise teacher, who died and has now risen from the dead."

Then Jesus spoke to them about how it was necessary for the Messiah to suffer before entering into his glory, and he explained all the places in the Scriptures that referred to him.

As they approached Emmaus they invited him to join them for a meal. So he went in to stay with them. When he was at table with them, he took bread, blessed and broke it, and gave it to them. Then their eyes were opened and they recognized him, and he vanished.

They said to each other, "Were not our hearts burning within us as he spoke to us along the road?"

Amazed, they got up and returned to Jerusalem to tell the others, "We have seen the Lord; he is indeed risen."

Adapted from Luke 24:13–35

**5 minutes**

**tip**

Let the children know you care. They will care more about what you are teaching if they know you care.

**Jesus said: I am the resurrection and the life. Anyone who believes in me, even though that person dies, will live, and whoever lives and believes in me will never die.**

John 11:25–26

## READ AND EXPLORE

### Step-by-Step

**1** Read the text out loud to the students. Be animated. The truth that Jesus is always with us is great news to share!

**My Notes:**

_____

_____

_____

_____

_____

_____

_____

_____

**We become the stories we listen to, read and tell.**

The Rhythm of Life

The risen Jesus is always at our side, but often we don't recognize him. Jesus is by our side when we wake up each morning, he is by our side when we are playing with friends, he is by our side when we are at baseball and ballet, he is by our side when we are doing our homework, he is by our side when we go shopping, and he is by our side when we go to bed at night.

In the morning, he is so excited for you to wake up and start a new day. At soccer he is cheering for you to do your best. And when you go shopping, he is whispering in your ear, "Is what you are about to buy going to help you become the-best-version-of-yourself?"

Jesus is present in a special way at Mass. The disciples had a powerful encounter with Jesus on the road to Emmaus, but you get to have an even more powerful encounter with him each Sunday at Mass. And very soon you are going to be able to receive Jesus in the Eucharist.

3 minutes

**tip**
Be patient. When a student behaves poorly, display an attitude of caring and concern. Do your best to avoid coming across as frustrated or annoyed. Try to redirect his or her behavior to a more desired result. For example: "It is not ok to talk while I am talking. Please wait until I have finished next time. Thank you."

**If you wish to adore the real face of Jesus, we can find it in the divine Eucharist, where the Body and Blood of Jesus Christ, the face of our Lord is hidden under the white veil of the Host.**

St. Gaetano Catanoso

## WATCH AND EXPLORE

### Step-by-Step

 **1** Introduce Episode 6 by saying: "What is the greatest event on earth? Let's find out!"

**2** Watch Episode 6.

**3** Ask the children: "What is the greatest event on earth?"

- THE MASS!

**Wisdom is never old fashioned. Wisdom is truth lived.**

Decision Point

70

## So Many Wonders

There are so many wonderful things that happen during the Mass. If you went to Mass every day of your life, you would still be discovering its wonders at the end of your life. There is nothing like the Mass.

We have already talked about how God speaks to us at Mass. That is amazing. The Eucharist is another wonder we experience at Mass. We believe that during the Mass, a simple piece of bread and a cup of wine are transformed into the Body and Blood of Jesus. That is amazing!

It is amazing that God gives himself to us in this way. At Mass God gives himself to us completely in the Eucharist, and at Mass we give ourselves completely to him in prayer. We are going to talk a lot more about this in the coming pages.

Sometimes people say they are bored at Mass. Usually this is because they don't know what is going on or because they are not listening to what God is saying to them. It is impossible to be bored at Mass if we are trying to listen to God's voice. If we ever find Mass boring, it's time for us to put more energy into our conversation with God.

If we find Mass uninteresting, perhaps we need to learn more about what is actually happening. Everything that happens at Mass happens for a reason, and when we really know what is going on, it is fascinating.

**My Notes:**

_____

_____

_____

_____

_____

_____

_____

_____

Sometimes it helps to have a missal, a small book that explains everything that is happening in the Mass. It can be very helpful to follow along.

Another way to make sure we don't get bored at Mass is to sing all the songs and respond to all the prayers. When you participate in Mass you are in a conversation with God. It is only when we stop participating that we get bored. Plus, when we talk with God, he tells us amazing things!

As we grow in wisdom we discover that the Mass is the most amazing event on earth!

**10 minutes**

**tip**

When possible, get some feedback from the children. What is their favorite part of the Mass? When do they feel closest to God at Mass? Do they ever think about all the Christians who have been to Mass since the time of Jesus? From time to time, it helps to get in the mind of the children you serve. Learning more about the children will help you address their specific questions and serve them in powerful ways.

**It would be easier for the world to survive without the sun than to do without Holy Mass.**

St. Pio of Pietrelcina

## SHOW WHAT YOU KNOW

### Step-by-Step

**1** Have the children complete the activity page by themselves, with a partner, or as a group.

**2** After three minutes, ask the class: "Are there any questions you are struggling with?"

**3** Briefly explain the answers to any questions they might have, referring back to the specific page in the workbook.

**Jesus never asked, "What's in it for me?" He was not motivated by the individualist creed; he was motivated by a spirit of service.**

Rediscover Catholicism

# Show What You Know

### True or False

1. __T__ Your First Communion is going to be a very special day in your life. (p 55)

2. __F__ God wants you to live the worst life imaginable. (p 56)

3. __T__ The Ten Commandments show us the best way to live. (p 58)

4. __F__ God never speaks to us. (p 60)

5. __T__ Every Sunday at church God has something he wants to tell you. (p 61)

### Fill in the blank

1. Each Sunday God invites us over to his _____house_____ for a great celebration. (p 57)

2. The _____mass_____ is one of the greatest blessings God gives us as Catholics. (p 54)

3. The Eucharist is a _____celebration_____ of God's love for us. (p 55)

4. When we spend time with God he fills us with _____grace_____ so that we can live holy lives. (p 57)

5. The Ten Commandments are a _____blessing_____ God gives us to help us become the-best-version-of-ourselves. (p 58)

**My Notes:**

_____

_____

_____

_____

_____

_____

_____

_____

6. It is _____**impossible**_____ to be bored at Mass if we are trying to listen to God's voice. (p 70)

7. The Mass is the _____**ultimate**_____ prayer. (p 55)

8. Learning to _____**listen**_____ to God's voice is one of the most important lessons we can learn in life. (p 60)

9. If you went to Mass every day of your life, you would still be discovering its _____**wonders**_____ at the end of your life. (p 70)

10. As you grow in wisdom you discover that the Mass is the most _____**amazing**_____ event on earth. (p 71)

**Word Bank**

HOUSE  AMAZING  CELEBRATION  IMPOSSIBLE  GRACE
MASS  ULTIMATE  LISTEN  WONDERS  BLESSING

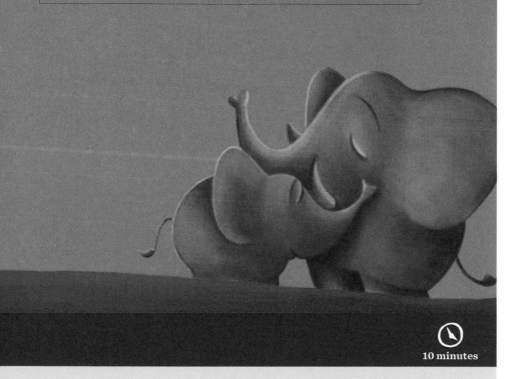

10 minutes

**tip**

If you are running short on time, you may choose to complete this section together as a class. Simply read each fill-in-the-blank and true-and--false statement and invite your students to call out the answer. Once someone calls out the right answer, ask everyone to write it down in their workbooks. If you are completely out of time, ask the children to complete the exercise for homework.

**Remember that when you leave this earth, you can take nothing that you received—only what you have been given: a full heart, enriched by honest service, love, sacrifice, and courage.**

St. Francis of Assisi

# JOURNAL WITH JESUS

### Step-by-Step

**1** Invite the children to write a letter to Jesus.

**2** Ask them to remain silent during their journaling time.

**3** You may wish to play some quiet, reflective music to help create the right mood in the classroom and to encourage the students to remain quiet and focused on journaling with Jesus.

**Beyond life's complexities, there is simplicity. Beneath the chaos and confusion of life, there is understanding. It is the Gospel, the good news.**

Rediscover Catholicism

**My Notes:**

_____

_____

_____

_____

_____

_____

_____

_____

_____

## Journal with Jesus

Dear Jesus,

I am excited to receive you in the Eucharist for the first time because . . .

_____

_____

_____

_____

_____

_____

_____

_____

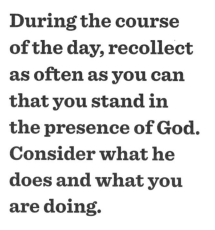

**10 minutes**

_____

_____

_____

_____

_____

_____

**tip**

Walk around while they are writing. This action will help each child stay more focused and will also allow you to help with any questions they might have.

**During the course of the day, recollect as often as you can that you stand in the presence of God. Consider what he does and what you are doing.**

St. Francis de Sales

# CLOSING PRAYER

## Step-by-Step

**1** Prepare the children to pray with Ben. Get them settled and quiet.

**2** Watch Episode 7.

**3** Ask the children: "What are some of the most important things you learned in this session?"

- THE MASS IS THE MOST AMAZING EVENT ON EARTH.

- EVERY SUNDAY, GOD HAS A SPECIAL MESSAGE FOR ME.

- JESUS IS PRESENT IN A SPECIAL WAY AT MASS ON SUNDAY.

- WHEN I SPEND TIME WITH GOD, HE FILLS ME WITH HIS GRACE SO THAT I CAN LIVE A HOLY LIFE.

- LEARNING TO LISTEN TO GOD'S VOICE IS ONE OF THE MOST IMPORTANT LESSONS WE CAN LEARN IN LIFE.

## Closing Prayer

Tragically, there are many people who spend their whole lives not knowing Jesus and how much he loves them. This is very sad.

The reason they never meet Jesus is because they never go looking for him. God speaks to us in many ways. He speaks to us through the Church, the Bible, the Mass, nature, great art and literature, and one another. But to hear God, to meet him, to discover his amazing plan for your life, you need to seek him!

Let's pray together now and ask God to give us the courage and the desire to always seek him, no matter what:

> Be, Lord Jesus,
> a bright flame before me,
> a guiding star above me,
> a smooth path below me,
> a kindly shepherd behind me:
> today, tonight, and forever.
>
> Amen.

Prayer of St. Columba

**My Notes:**

_____

_____

_____

_____

_____

_____

_____

5 minutes

**To fall in love with God is the greatest romance; to seek him the greatest adventure; to find him, the greatest human achievement.**

St. Augustine of Hippo

# 3

# The Word of God

## QUICK SESSION OVERVIEW

Opening Prayer. . . . . . . . . . . . . . . . . . . . . . . . . . . . . . . . . . . 4 min

Watch and Discuss; Read and Explore . . . . . . . . . . . . . 73 min

Show What You Know . . . . . . . . . . . . . . . . . . . . . . . . . . . 5 min

Journal with Jesus. . . . . . . . . . . . . . . . . . . . . . . . . . . . . . . 5 min

Closing Prayer. . . . . . . . . . . . . . . . . . . . . . . . . . . . . . . . . . 3 min

## OBJECTIVES

- **TO PROCLAIM** that two of the ways God reveals his amazing plan for our lives are through the Bible and Mass on Sunday.

- **TO EXPLAIN** that Jesus is the greatest teacher who ever lived.

- **TO TEACH** that we gather at church with our family, friends, and all our parish family to worship God in the way that Jesus taught us to.

# • Setting aside weekly prep time.
# • Seeking counsel.

## WELCOME

Jesus is the greatest teacher who ever walked the earth. His teaching method has inspired countless pages of analysis and thousands of hours of training. Here are two methods Jesus used to be a great leader.

### JESUS PREPARED FOR THE WORK ENTRUSTED TO HIM BY GOD.

Jesus underwent an intense period of preparation before beginning his public ministry. After being baptized in the Jordan River by John the Baptist, Jesus prayed and fasted for forty days and forty nights alone in the desert. Why? Because Jesus knew that preparation is essential.

Preparation dramatically increases the quality of the experience for both the student and the teacher. Without it, leaders struggle to engage their students, respond effectively to questions, or even enjoy themselves.

### JESUS DIDN'T WORK ALONE.

Over and over again throughout the Gospels, we read about Jesus retreating to a quiet place seeking counsel from God the Father. He did it before choosing his disciples, before feeding of the 5,000, and before returning to Jerusalem to face crucifixion and death.

You don't have to lead this class by yourself. Seek wisdom from others. Most of all, pray, because no one wants you to be successful more than God.

**Prayer Icon**

**Read and Explore**

**Watch and Discuss**

**Show What You Know**

**Journal with Jesus**

**Time Tracker**

## OPENING PRAYER

### Step-by-Step

**1** Gather students for prayer. Wait for them to be quiet. Don't rush this . . . reverence takes patience and practice.

**2** Before reading the prayer out loud, take a deep breath to allow an additional moment of silence. You never know what God might say to your students (or you!) when given the opportunity.

**3** Pray!

**Developing a dynamic prayer life requires perseverance more than anything else.**

Decision Point

**My Notes:**

_____

_____

_____

_____

_____

_____

_____

# 3
# The Word of God

God, our loving Father,
thank you for all the ways you bless me.
Help me to be aware that every person,
place, and adventure I experience is an
opportunity to love you more.
Fill me with a desire to change and to grow,
and give me the grace to become
the-best-version-of-myself in
every moment of every day.

Amen.

**4 minutes**

**tip**

Prayer is as easy as
one-two-three!

1. Bow your head
   (show respect for God.)
2. Close your eyes
   (focus the mind.)
3. Fold your hands
   (still body.)

If your students need
help, model it for them
first and then practice it.
It's amazing how many
kids struggle with prayer
because they struggle
with their posture. Finally,
begin the prayer with "In
the name of the Father,
and of the Son, and of
the Holy Spirit."

**But seek first his
kingdom and his
righteousness,
and all of these
things will be given
unto you as well.**

Matthew 6:33

## WATCH AND DISCUSS

**Step-by-Step**

**1** Introduce Episode 1 by saying: "Ben is put to the test by his friends. Will he pass the test? Let's watch to find out!"

**2** Watch Episode 1.

**The human person cannot live without meaning and purpose.**

The Rhythm of Life

# Overview of the Mass

Each time you go to Mass there are many things that happen. Behind each prayer and each action is enormous meaning; everything in the Mass happens for a reason. In our spiritual journey as Catholics we are always uncovering new layers of meaning, so we never stop learning about the Mass.

The Mass is made up of four parts:

1. **The Introductory Rites**
2. **The Liturgy of the Word**
3. **The Liturgy of the Eucharist**
4. **The Concluding Rites**

There are two words for us to pay special attention to here: rite and liturgy.

**My Notes:**

_____

_____

_____

_____

_____

_____

_____

## What Is a Rite?

A rite is something that is said or done the same way every time for a reason. For example, the Sign of the Cross is a rite. We do it the same way every time. We say it the same way every time: "In the name of the Father, and of the Son, and of the Holy Spirit. Amen."

The order is for a reason. God the Father is the first person of the Blessed Trinity. God the Son is the second person of the Holy Trinity. And God the Holy Spirit is the third person of the Holy Trinity.

If you went to Mass and the priest began by making the Sign of the Cross and saying, "In the name of the Son, and of the Holy Spirit, and of the Father. Amen," you would know that something was wrong.

Our Catholic faith has many rites. Each rite has a reason.

**8 minutes**

**tip**

Intentionally compliment the children. Instead of a general praising of an accomplishment, encourage persistence. For example, "Toni, you paid great attention to that episode. Thank you." A simple statement like that will go a long way in replicating positive habits.

I am but an instrument, a tiny pencil in the hands of the Lord with which he writes what he likes. However imperfect we are, he writes beautifully.

St. Teresa of Calcutta

## READ AND EXPLORE

### Step-by-Step

**1** Invite the children to look at the illustration and ask: "Do you recognize anything?"

- THE CUP THE PRIEST IS HOLDING: *CHALICE*
- THE OUTER GARMENT WORN BY THE PRIEST: *CHASUBLE*
- THE NAME OF THE BROWN BOX BEHIND THE PRIEST: *THE ALTAR*
- THE NAME OF THE CLOTH ON TOP OF THE ALTAR: *THE ALTAR CLOTH*

**In all our lives there is a great danger in believing that who we are, where we are, and what we have is all that there is. There is more.**

The Rhythm of Life

### What Is Liturgy?

Liturgy is a prayer we participate in as a community. During the Mass we experience two types of liturgy: the Liturgy of the Word and the Liturgy of the Eucharist.

During the Liturgy of the Word we listen to readings from the Bible and a homily from the priest or deacon, then we pray the Creed together and offer our petitions to God.

During the Liturgy of the Eucharist we offer our lives and our gifts to God, prepare the altar, pray the Eucharistic Prayer, and receive Holy Communion.

Liturgy is a beautiful way to spend time with God and our parish family.

**My Notes:**

_____

_____

_____

_____

_____

_____

_____

## Where Do We Celebrate Mass?

We celebrate Mass at church. Our parish church is a very special place because it is God's house. We gather at church with our family, friends, and all our parish family to worship God in the way that Jesus taught us to.

The Mass is a beautiful ritual made up of prayers, liturgies, and rites. During the Mass we use many special items to help us celebrate. Do you recognize any of these items?

5 minutes

**And when he had given thanks, he broke it and said, "This is my body, that is for you; do this in remembrance of me."**

1 Corinthians 11:24

## WATCH AND DISCUSS

### Step-by-Step

**1** Introduce Episode 2 by saying: "What do you think is the most amazing thing Fr. Tom has ever seen?"

**2** Watch Episode 2.

**3** Ask the children: "What is the most amazing thing that Fr. Tom has ever seen?"

- DURING THE MASS, THE BREAD AND WINE TURN INTO THE BODY AND BLOOD OF JESUS!

**Christ invites us to a life of discipline not for his sake, but for our sake; not to help him, but to help us; not to make him happy, but to allow us to share in his happiness.**

Rediscover Catholicism

## The Introductory Rites

We come to church on Sunday to celebrate Mass. It's a great way to thank God for all the blessings he has given us.

During the Mass we remember Jesus' life, death, and Resurrection, and the most amazing thing happens, something that doesn't happen anywhere else: the priest changes bread and wine into the Body and Blood of Jesus.

How can he do this? God gives priests special powers. At your First Reconciliation God forgave your sins through the priest. During Mass God transforms the bread and wine into the Body and Blood of Jesus through the priest.

Another amazing thing that happens at church is that we get to receive Holy Communion. We get to receive Jesus in the Eucharist. This is an amazing blessing.

When you go back to your pew after you receive Jesus in the Eucharist, kneel down, close your eyes, and pray. This is a very special moment because God is inside you.

Now let's talk about the four parts of the Mass. Do you remember what they are?

1. **The Introductory Rites**
2. **The Liturgy of the Word**
3. **The Liturgy of the Eucharist**
4. **The Concluding Rites**

**My Notes:**

_____

_____

_____

_____

_____

_____

_____

## The Introductory Rites

Mass begins with this procession. The priest, deacon, readers, and altar servers walk together in procession toward the altar. This procession is usually accompanied by music. Music helps us to raise our hearts to God in praise and thanksgiving.

Have you ever noticed that music can make you very joyful? This is your heart and soul leaping for joy. Music is a powerful way to pray. Saint Augustine said, "Singing is like praying twice."

Once the priest gets to the altar he begins with the Sign of the Cross: "In the name of the Father, and of the Son, and of the Holy Spirit. Amen."

The Sign of the Cross is a rite.

**9 minutes**

**We should spend as much time in thanking God for his benefits as we do in asking him for them.**

St. Vincent de Paul

85

**Step-by-Step**

**1** Invite the children to explore the illustration.

**2** Inform the children that the image depicts the story of the woman at the well. If time allows, read the story. It can be found in the fourth chapter of John's Gospel, verses 1–42.

**Our peace is founded not on our perfection but on God's mercy. Call on his mercy.**

Mustard Seeds

# We Say Sorry

God loves healthy relationships, and a very important part of healthy relationships is saying sorry when we do or say something that hurts the other person. Catholics say sorry. The reason is because our friendship with God and our friendships with each other cannot thrive if we don't say sorry.

If you were playing on the playground with a friend yesterday and he pushed you over and didn't say sorry, how would you feel? You might wonder if he was really your friend. But if he came up to you and the first thing he did was say, "I'm sorry I pushed you over yesterday. I won't do it again. Please forgive me."

How would that make you feel? You would be reminded that he really does want to be your friend.

That's why, after the Sign of the Cross, the first thing we do at Mass is say sorry to God. We want him to know that we are his friends and that we want to be really good friends to him.

We say sorry to God and ask for forgiveness at the beginning of Mass with a really simple and beautiful prayer:

**Priest: Lord Have Mercy**
**Congregation: Lord Have Mercy**
**Priest: Christ Have Mercy**
**Congregation: Christ Have Mercy**
**Priest: Lord Have Mercy**
**Congregation: Lord Have Mercy**

**My Notes:**

_____

_____

_____

_____

_____

_____

_____

_____

5 minutes

**If you do not believe Christ's mercy is enough to forgive the worst sins, then you commit an unforgivable sin against the Holy Spirit.**

Venerable Fulton Sheen

## READ AND EXPLORE

### Step-by-Step

**1** Ask the children: "Do you know where the first line of the Gloria comes from?"

**2** If they don't know, give them a hint: "The answer can be found by looking at the illustration!"

**3** If they still don't know, share with them the answer.

- THE ANGEL WHO ANNOUNCED TO THE SHEPHERDS THAT JESUS WAS BORN GREETED THE SHEPHERDS BY SAYING, "GLORY TO GOD IN THE HIGHEST AND ON EARTH PEACE TO PEOPLE OF GOOD WILL." LUKE 2:14

**Our best days are those when we stay connected with God throughout the day.**

Rediscover Jesus

# Glory to God

Next we say or sing The Gloria.

At different times in life we pray for different reasons. And at different times in the Mass we pray for different reasons.

Sometimes we pray to ask God to help us. This is called a prayer of petition. Sometimes we pray to ask God to help other people. This is called a prayer of intercession. Sometimes we pray to thank God for all the ways he has blessed us. This is called a prayer of thanksgiving. And sometimes we pray to praise God for his goodness. This is called a prayer of praise.

The Gloria is a prayer of praise. Sometimes we sing it and sometimes we say it, but always for the same reason —to praise God!

**My Notes:**

_____

_____

_____

_____

_____

_____

_____

Glory to God in the highest,
and on earth peace to people of good will.
We praise you, we bless you, we adore you, we glorify you.
We give you thanks for your great glory,
Lord God, heavenly King,
O God, almighty Father.
Lord Jesus Christ, Only Begotten Son, Lord God,
Lamb of God, Son of the Father,
You take away the sins of the world, have mercy on us;
You take away the sins of the world, receive our prayer;
You are seated at the right hand of the Father, have mercy on us.
For you alone are the Holy One,
You alone are the Lord,
You alone are the Most High, Jesus Christ,
With the Holy Spirit, in the glory of God the Father. Amen.

After the Gloria, the priest reads the opening prayer from the
Roman Missal. Then the whole congregation responds with
"Amen," and we sit down to listen to the Word of God.

5 minutes

**I am not capable of doing big things, but I want to do everything, even the smallest things, for the greater glory of God.**

St. Dominic Savio

## WATCH AND DISCUSS

### Step-by-Step

**1** Introduce Episode 3 by saying: "Fr. Tom asked Ben to help him with a very special task. Let's find out what it is!"

**2** Watch Episode 3.

**Your happiness in this life and the next depends in large part on how seriously you take the Word of God.**

Decision Point

# The Liturgy of the Word

During the part of the Mass we call the Liturgy of the Word, we listen to the Word of God and reflect on how we can live our lives as God invites us to.

The Liturgy of the Word includes readings from the Bible, the homily, the Creed, and the intercessory prayers.

At Mass on Sunday we listen to four readings from the Bible:

1. **The First Reading, from the Old Testament**
2. **The Responsorial Psalm**
3. **The Second Reading, from the New Testament**
4. **The Gospel Reading, from one of the four Gospels: Matthew, Mark, Luke, and John**

Each reading is specifically selected to connect with a theme that the Church wants us to reflect on that week. And guess what: Every Catholic parish reads the same readings each Sunday.

**My Notes:**

_____

_____

_____

_____

_____

_____

_____

_____

So if you have a friend on the other side of the country, you can talk about the readings because they heard the same ones you heard at Mass.

Different people read different readings. Perhaps one day you will become a reader at Mass. There are so many ways to be involved in the life of the parish—reading at Mass is just one of them.

You are a layperson. A layperson is an unordained member of the Church, and he or she usually reads the First Reading, the Responsorial Psalm, and the Second Reading. The priest or the deacon reads the Gospel. Both the priest and deacon are ordained members of the Church.

5 minutes

**tip**

If time allows, take a moment to share about the importance of being involved in the parish. Perhaps highlight how special it is to be a reader at Mass. The children are likely too young to be a reader now, but by building up a level of excitement around the idea you will plant an important seed in the hearts of the children.

**Courageously follow the path of personal holiness and diligently nourish yourselves with the Word of God and the Eucharist. The holier you are, the more you can contribute to building up the Church and society.**

St. John Paul II

91

## READ AND EXPLORE

**Step-by-Step**

**1** Activity: FOLLOW THE LEADER!
Invite all of the children to stand up and face you. Request that the children "follow the leader" and do everything you do. Then run in place, do jumping jacks and arm circles, stretch by touching your toes and then reaching as high as the sky, and make up your own unique moves for the children to follow. Have fun with this!

**God's plea to humanity has always been a call to go within and discover the truth about ourselves, which is that we have been created in the image and likeness of God.**

Mustard Seeds

Some parishes don't have Mass every Sunday because there are not enough priests. This is very sad. Some Sundays these parishes have to have Eucharistic services instead of Mass. During a Eucharistic service we still listen to the readings of the Mass and the Eucharist is distributed from the tabernacle. In this case a layperson can read the Gospel.

After the Gospel, the priest or deacon delivers the homily. During the homily, the priest or deacon explains the readings, shows us how they apply to our lives, and inspires us to live what we have just heard from God's Word.

**My Notes:**

_____

_____

_____

_____

_____

_____

_____

8 minutes

**tip**

During the activity play music to accompany the moment. Select something that is upbeat and fun. If you have *Blessed: A Collection of Songs for the Young at Heart*, it's recommended to play "It's a Beautiful Day." Movement helps students to focus and it's fun!

**Give thanks to the God of heaven, for his steadfast love endures forever.**

Psalm 136:26

93

## WATCH AND DISCUSS

### Step-by-Step

**1** Introduce Episode 4 with some excitement by saying: "I am so excited to share this episode with you! Sarah is going to take us on a journey through the Creed and it's awesome. Let's watch together."

**2** Watch Episode 4.

**3** Have the children share with someone next to them the one thing that stuck out during the episode. When they are done, share the one thing that stuck out to you. Be excited when you do. This is cool stuff! And your voice should reflect that.

**Only one thing is necessary for Catholicism to flourish: authentic lives.**

Rediscover Catholicism

## We Believe

After the homily, we stand and proclaim the Creed together, and then we have the prayers of the faithful.

Everyone believes something. There are many things we believe as Catholics. We believe in God, we believe God loves us, we believe God has blessed us, and we believe in the power of prayer. But there are many other things we believe.

At Mass each Sunday we proclaim the Creed. The Creed is a summary of the core beliefs that make up our Catholic faith.

**My Notes:**

_____

_____

_____

_____

_____

_____

_____

_____

**3 minutes**

I know this now. Every man gives his life for what he believes. Every woman gives her life for what she believes. Sometimes people believe in little or nothing, and yet they give their lives to that little or nothing. One life is all we have and we live it as we believe in living it and then it's gone. But to surrender what you are and to live without belief is more terrible than dying —even more terrible than dying young.

St. Joan of Arc

95

## READ AND EXPLORE

### Step-by-Step

**1** Invite a different student to read each line of the Creed out loud. If you don't have thirty students in the class, keep cycling through the group until you finish.

**2** The children may have difficulty reading the different style fonts or pronouncing some of the bigger words. Be ready to help them sound out any particularly difficult words or supply the word.

**When you come to recognize and believe that you are a son or daughter of God you will also become aware that you lack absolutely nothing.**

Mustard Seeds

*The Creed*

I BELIEVE IN ONE GOD, **THE FATHER ALMIGHTY,**

*maker of heaven and earth*

AND ALL THINGS VISIBLE AND INVISIBLE.

**I BELIEVE IN ONE LORD JESUS CHRIST,**

THE ONLY BEGOTTEN SON OF GOD, BORN OF THE FATHER BEFORE ALL AGES.

GOD FROM GOD, LIGHT FROM LIGHT,

**TRUE GOD FROM TRUE GOD,**

BEGOTTEN, NOT MADE, CONSUBSTANTIAL WITH THE FATHER;

THROUGH HIM ALL THINGS WERE MADE.

FOR US MEN AND FOR OUR SALVATION HE CAME DOWN FROM HEAVEN,

**AND BY THE HOLY SPIRIT**

*was incarnate of the Virgin Mary*

**AND BECAME MAN.**

FOR OUR SAKE HE WAS CRUCIFIED UNDER PONTIUS PILATE,

HE SUFFERED DEATH AND WAS BURIED,

**My Notes:**

_____

_____

_____

_____

_____

_____

_____

_____

and rose again on the third day

in accordance with the Scriptures.

**HE ASCENDED INTO HEAVEN**

**AND IS SEATED AT THE RIGHT HAND OF THE FATHER.**

HE WILL COME AGAIN IN GLORY

to judge the living and the dead

**AND HIS KINGDOM WILL HAVE NO END.**

I believe in the Holy Spirit, the Lord, the giver of life,

**WHO PROCEEDS FROM THE FATHER AND THE SON,**

who with the Father and the Son is adored and glorified,

who has spoken through the prophets.

**I BELIEVE IN ONE, HOLY, CATHOLIC AND APOSTOLIC CHURCH.**

I confess one Baptism for the forgiveness of sins

**and I look forward to the resurrection of the dead**

AND THE LIFE OF THE WORLD TO COME.

*Amen.*

**5 minutes**

**tip**

Stay positive. God has allowed you to teach the faith to his children. Be careful not to discourage questions or punish doubt; instead, see these as invitations of the Holy Spirit to explore and study the faith more. If time allows, ask the children if they have any questions about the Creed. Don't worry about not having all the answers. You can always write the question down, look up the answer, and then provide the answer next class. The important thing is to let them know that questions are a good thing and, even more importantly, that the Church has deeply personal answers to their deeply personal questions.

**Who is it that overcomes the world? Only the one who believes that Jesus is the Son of God.**

1 John 5:5

## WATCH AND DISCUSS

### Step-by-Step

**1** Introduce Episode 5 by saying: "I hope you are as excited as I am for the parable of the sower to come to life. *Hint:* Watch closely what happens to the seeds."

**2** Watch Episode 5.

**Catholicism is a dynamic way of life designed by God to help you explore your incredible potential.**

Rediscover Catholicism

## From the Bible: The Sower of Seeds

As Jesus made his way from village to village, word about his great deeds spread very quickly. He became very famous as a great teacher and healer, and so everywhere he went huge crowds of people would gather around him.

One day Jesus was sitting by the lake, and a large crowd gathered around him. They wanted him to teach them and heal them. So Jesus sat in a boat at the water's edge, the people stood around, and he told them parables. One of those parables was about a farmer sowing seeds.

**My Notes:**

_____

_____

_____

_____

_____

_____

_____

_____

A farmer went out to sow seeds in his field. As he sowed the seeds, some fell on the path beside the field, and birds came down and ate them. Other seeds fell on rocky ground, where there was not sufficient soil. These seeds sprang up quickly, but because of the shallow soil, when the sun rose it scorched them and they died. Still other seeds fell among thorns, and as they grew they were choked by the thorns. But some seeds fell on the rich, good soil, and these grew strong and healthy, and brought forth an abundant harvest.

God is the farmer. Our hearts and souls are the soil. The world, selfishness, and evil are the birds, the thorns, and the scorching hot sun. Daily prayer, learning about our faith, going to Mass on Sunday, being generous to all who cross our path, and sharing God's message with others all help to make your heart and soul like the rich soil that receives the seed and produces an abundant harvest.

Adapted from Matthew 13:1–9

🕐
**5 minutes**

**tip**
Perspective is powerful. There are going to be moments when you want to express your impatience with the children. It will probably come after having to tell them to quiet down for the 5000th time before watching an episode of the animation. You'll want to reprimand them and that's natural. But when you feel that way, consider your own relationship with God. How many times has God had to remind you of something? How many times has he showed you loving kindness only for you to turn around repeat the same careless mistakes over and over again, sometimes even on purpose? God's mercy and his patience are thankfully endless, and he invites you to care for your students in the same way.

**Who except God can give you peace? Has the world ever been able to satisfy the heart?**

St. Gerard Majella

99

## WATCH AND DISCUSS

### Step-by-Step

**1** Introduce Episode 6 by saying: "In this episode, Hemingway finds a secret passage way in the clubhouse. Let's see where it leads!"

**2** Watch Episodes 6.

**True fulfillment can only be found in and through Jesus Christ. You cannot become the-best-version-of-yourself except in and through Jesus.**

Decision Point

100

## Wear It Out

All of the readings at Mass come from the most famous book in the world: the Bible. It is the best-selling book of all time. When you pick up the Bible it may seem like you are holding one big book, but in fact, it is a collection of 73 books.

The Bible is made up of two main sections: the Old Testament and the New Testament. There are 46 books in the Old Testament and 27 books in the New Testament.

One of the many ways God speaks to us is through the Bible. God has an amazing plan for your life, and one of the ways he reveals that amazing plan is through the readings we hear at Mass every Sunday.

If you were going on a long journey it would be a good idea to take a map with you. It would be even better to take a guide with you who has made the journey before. The Bible is like that map and

**My Notes:**

_____

_____

_____

_____

_____

_____

_____

_____

the Church is like that guide to help you make your journey through this life into the next so that you can live with God in heaven forever.

Over and over throughout the Bible God speaks to people, guiding them, encouraging them, and warning them. He spoke to Adam and Eve, Moses and Abraham, Noah and Jacob, Rebecca and Ruth, Mary and Paul. God spoke to each of them in different ways, but he spoke to them all. And now, God wants to speak to you.

Jesus is the central figure in the Bible. In the Old Testament we read over and over again about how the people were waiting for Jesus, the Messiah, to come. The New Testament is about Jesus and his teachings and about the life of the early Church and how the first Christians tried to live the Gospel message.

I have had some wonderful teachers in my life, and I am sure you have too. Jesus is the greatest teacher who ever lived. His favorite way to teach was to tell stories. He told stories that ordinary people could understand.

Do you have a favorite Bible story?

**10 minutes**

**tip**
Take a moment and share with the children your favorite Bible story.

**The Lord himself goes before you and will be with you; he will never leave you nor forsake you. Do not be afraid; do not be discouraged.**

Deuteronomy 31:8

101

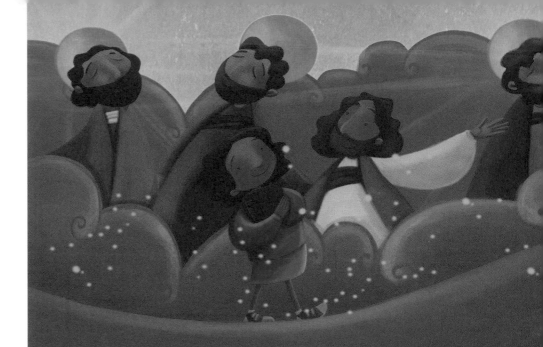

## READ AND EXPLORE

### Step-by-Step

**1** Beginning from the last paragraph on page 102 read the text out loud to the children.

**2** Ask the children, "Do you want Jesus to be one of your best friends? How about the saints?"

Do you have a favorite shirt or sweater? Do you have a favorite pair of shoes? I have an old sweatshirt that I just love. It is all worn out. The color is fading and there are a couple of holes in it, but it is so comfortable. It has been with me in good times and in bad times, and it comforts me in ways that a new sweatshirt cannot.

Many years ago a good friend inspired and challenged me. He said, "One of my goals in life is to wear out a Bible." I thought to myself, "What a fabulous goal."

Now I want to challenge you. Get yourself a Bible to carry with you throughout your life. Ask your parents or grandparents to

**Life is wonderful but brief. Each day is filled with unimaginable potential. The life God invites us to allows us to live each moment consciously and with vibrant enthusiasm.**

Rediscover Catholicism.

**My Notes:**

_____

_____

_____

_____

_____

_____

_____

read a little to you each day. As you get older, read a little yourself each day. Wear that Bible out by reading it, reflecting on what you learn, and praying for the grace to live what you learn.

Over a lifetime Jesus and the other great people in the Bible will become great friends of yours. They will teach you how to grow in virtue, become the-best-version-of-yourself, and live a holy life.

Somewhere down the road, I hope we meet, and when we do, I hope you will show me your worn-out Bible.

God wants you to have many companions on your journey to heaven. He wants you to have friends who help you become the-best-version-of-yourself. But he also wants you to be friends with the saints because they have already made this journey and can teach you so much about which path to take and the paths to avoid. God also gives us our guardian angels to accompany us on the journey. And God gives us the Bible and the Church as great companions along the way too.

**5 minutes**

---

---

---

---

---

---

---

---

**tip**

What is your relationship with the Bible? For many, the Bible is just a collection of stories they have heard many times before. After all, it is so easy to think that we know a certain story, and to tune out as a result. But to do so would be a mistake. The Word of God is constantly new and fresh, even for those who have spent a lifetime exploring it. The reason is because our lives are constantly changing, we are constantly changing, and our relationship with God and others is constantly changing. If you have not yet had a life-changing experience with the Bible, I am excited for the opportunity you have before you.

**For the word of God is alive and active. Sharper than any double-edged sword, it penetrates even to dividing soul and spirit, joints and marrow; it judges the thoughts and attitudes of the heart.**

Hebrews 4:12

## SHOW WHAT YOU KNOW

### Step-by-Step

**1** Have your children complete the activity page by themselves, with a partner, or as a group.

**2** After three minutes ask the class: "Are there any questions you are struggling with?"

**3** Briefly explain the answer to any questions they might have, referring back to the specific page in the workbook.

**Follow your conscience and the guidance of the Holy Spirit and you will notice that you are less anxious and more joyful.**

Decision Point

## Show What You Know

### True or False

1. __T__ The Bible is a great companion for your journey to heaven. (p 101)

2. __F__ We should never say sorry even when we've done something wrong. (p 86)

3. __F__ There is no purpose or meaning behind each prayer and each action at Mass. (p 80)

4. __T__ God speaks to you through the Bible. (p 100)

5. __T__ Jesus is the greatest teacher who ever lived. (p 101)

### Fill in the blank

1. God has an amazing _____plan_____ for your life. (p 100)

2. Our parish church is a very special place because it is God's _____house_____. (p 83)

3. God reveals his amazing plan for your life through the _____readings_____ you hear at Mass every Sunday. (p 100)

4. Going to Mass on Sunday is a great way to thank God for all the _____blessings_____ he has given you. (p 84)

5. At Mass we get to receive_____Jesus_____ in the Eucharist. (p 84)

**My Notes:**

_____

_____

_____

_____

_____

_____

_____

_____

6. Music helps us to raise our hearts to God in _____praise_____ and _____thanksgiving_____. (p 85)

7. God loves _____healthy_____ relationships. (p 86)

8. The _____Bible_____ is the most famous book in the world. (p 100)

9. One of the many ways God _____speaks_____ to you is through the Bible. (p 100)

10. The Bible is your _____map_____ and the Church is your _____guide_____ on your journey to live with God in heaven forever. (p 100–101)

**Word Bank**

THANKSGIVING   HOUSE   GUIDE   HEALTHY   SPEAKS   PRAISE   PLAN
READINGS   MAP   BIBLE   JESUS   BLESSINGS

**5 minutes**

**tip**
If you are running short on time, you may choose to complete this section together as a class. Simply read each fill-in-the blank and true-and-false statement and invite your students to call out the answer. Once someone calls out the right answer, ask everyone to write it down in their workbook. If you are completely out of time, ask the children to complete the exercise for homework.

**The goal of our life is to live with God forever. God, who loves us, gave us life. Our own response of love allows God's life to flow into us without limit.**

St. Ignatius of Loyola

105

# JOURNAL WITH JESUS

### Step-by-Step

**1** Invite your children to write a letter to Jesus.

**2** Ask the children to remain silent during their journaling time.

**3** You may wish to play some quiet, reflective music to help create the right mood in the classroom and to encourage the students to remain quiet and focused on journaling with Jesus.

**The way we respond to everything that happens in our lives causes us to either love more or less.**

Rediscover Jesus

**My Notes:**

_____

_____

_____

_____

_____

_____

_____

_____

# Journal with Jesus

Dear Jesus,

You are the greatest teacher in history; I need your help understanding . . .

_____

_____

_____

_____

_____

_____

_____

_____

🕐
**5 minutes**

_____

_____

_____

_____

_____

_____

**tip**

The children in front of you can grasp a lot more than you think. They might complain saying, "I don't know what to say!" Treat this as an opportunity to brainstorm as a group. Here are three prompts to help spark the brainstorm:

- MAKE A LIST OF THINGS YOU WANT TO SAY THANK YOU FOR.
- TELL JESUS WHEN YOU ARE AFRAID AND ASK HIM TO BE NEAR YOU.
- WRITE TO JESUS ABOUT SOMEONE WHO IS SICK AND IN NEED OF PRAYERS.

**The Lord your God is in your midst, a mighty one who will save; he will rejoice over you with gladness; he will quiet you by his love; he will exult over you with loud singing.**

Zephaniah 3:17

# CLOSING PRAYER

## Step-by-Step

**1** Prepare the children to pray with Ben. Get them settled and quiet.

**2** Watch Episode 7.

**3** Ask the children: "What are some of the most important things you learned in this session?"

- GOD REVEALS HIS AMAZING PLAN FOR OUR LIVES THROUGH THE BIBLE AND MASS ON SUNDAY.

- JESUS IS THE GREATEST TEACHER WHO EVER LIVED.

- ON SUNDAY WE WORSHIP GOD AS JESUS TAUGHT US.

- MASS IS A GREAT WAY TO THANK GOD FOR ALL THE BLESSINGS HE GIVES US.

- GOD LOVES HEALTHY RELATIONSHIPS.

## Closing Prayer

Throughout your life, you will come across many teachers. But none of them will ever love you more or possess greater wisdom than Jesus.

From time to time you will really want to become the-best-version-of-yourself, grow in virtue, and live a holy life but you won't know how to do it. Those are the moments when you go to Jesus, the greatest teacher who ever lived, and ask him for help.

St. Ignatius of Loyola was a great priest and teacher. He founded one of the largest and most influential religious orders in history, the Society of Jesus (better known as the Jesuits). He was a spiritual master because he knew how to ask Jesus for help.

Together let's use the words of St. Ignatius and ask God to teach us to become all he created us to be:

Lord, teach me to be generous. Teach me to serve you as you deserve; to give and not to count the cost, to fight and not to heed the wounds, to toil and not to seek for rest, to labor and not to ask for reward, save that of knowing that I do your will.

Amen.

**My Notes:**

_____

_____

_____

_____

_____

_____

_____

_____

3 minutes

**tip**

Are you praying for your students? And are you praying for the wisdom to lead this class effectively? Your potential influence on the children cannot be overstated. If you take a moment to think about it, in all likelihood, you can remember a teacher who had a really negative influence on you. He or she embarrassed you or made you feel like you were worth less than you are. At the same time, I am sure you can remember a teacher who inspired and encouraged you. In both cases, the teacher left a powerful impression on your life. This is an awesome responsibility that I am sure is not lost on you. The grace of God is your most powerful weapon in your efforts to positively influence the lives of these children. And the best way to call upon his grace is through prayer.

_____

_____

_____

_____

_____

_____

_____

**Seek the Lord and his strength; seek his presence continually!**

1 Chronicles 16:11

# The Eucharist

## QUICK SESSION OVERVIEW

Opening Prayer. . . . . . . . . . . . . . . . . . . . . . . . . . . . . . . . . . . . . . 4 min

Watch and Discuss; Read and Explore . . . . . . . . . . . . . 65 min

Show What You Know . . . . . . . . . . . . . . . . . . . . . . . . . . . . 8 min

Journal with Jesus . . . . . . . . . . . . . . . . . . . . . . . . . . . . . . . . 8 min

Closing Prayer. . . . . . . . . . . . . . . . . . . . . . . . . . . . . . . . . . . . . 5 min

## OBJECTIVES

- **TO PROCLAIM** that Jesus is truly present in the Eucharist.

- **TO EXPLAIN** that the Eucharist is food for our souls.

- **TO TEACH** that Holy Communion is a lifelong blessing
  we should never take for granted.

THERE WERE TWO TIMES WHEN PEOPLE FLED FROM JESUS . . .

# • **After his arrest and crucifixion.**
# • **After his teaching on the Eucharist.**

## WELCOME

Jesus said, "I am the bread of life...Unless you eat the flesh of the Son of man and drink his blood, you have no life in you" (John 6:48, 53).

Immediately after this, we read in the Gospel: "When many of his disciples heard it, they said, 'This is a difficult teaching; who can accept it?'" (John 6:60) And a few lines later we read, "After this, many of his disciples turned back and no longer followed him" (John 6:66).

Notice Jesus didn't say, "Oh, come back. I was only kidding. Let's talk about it. Maybe I was wrong. Perhaps we can change this teaching. We can work something out." No, he turned to his disciples, just as he turns to you and me today, and said, "Do you also wish to leave me?"

What is the one thing that's going to keep the children in front of you from fleeing Jesus just as many of the first disciples did? Belief in the true presence of the Eucharist.

**For that reason, this is the most important class you teach all year.**

**Prayer Icon**

**Read and Explore**

**Watch and Discuss**

**Show What You Know**

**Journal with Jesus**

**Time Tracker**

# OPENING PRAYER

### Step-by-Step

**1** Introduce the opening prayer by saying: "Let's take a moment in silence to be still and quiet and open ourselves up to whatever God wants to lead us to today."

**2** Make the Sign of the Cross together, deliberately. Read the opening prayer slowly and reflectively.

**Daily prayer is an opportunity to strengthen our connection with God.**

Decision Point

**My Notes:**

_____

_____

_____

_____

_____

_____

_____

_____

# 4
# The Eucharist

God, our loving Father,
thank you for all the ways you bless me.
Help me to be aware that every person,
place, and adventure I experience is an
opportunity to love you more.
Fill me with a desire to change and to grow,
and give me the grace to become
the-best-version-of-myself in
every moment of every day.

Amen.

4 minutes

**tip**
Thank the children for coming. Tell them you are happy to see them. Tell them that this is going to be a very special class and it is extremely important for them to pay special attention to the animated episodes, the pages in the workbook, and everything you have to say. Tell them how excited you are to share this class with them. Ask for their best listening ears. If they do . . . they will learn something amazing!

**This is the confidence we have in approaching God: that if we ask anything according to his will, he hears us.**

1 John 5:14

## WATCH AND DISCUSS

### Step-by-Step

**1** Introduce Episode 1 by saying: "Get ready to find out what happens when Ben forgets to feed Hemingway! *Hint:* it involves Ben's shoe, cheese, and very sharp teeth!"

**2** Watch Episode 1.

**3** Ask: "Sarah mentions six ways to feed your soul. What are they?"

- WORD OF GOD, THE EUCHARIST, PRAYER, SERVICE, SCRIPTURE, AND OUR FAITH COMMUNITY

**In the Eucharist, Jesus fuels and empowers his Church.**

Confessions of a Mega-Church Pastor

# Food for the Soul

God has blessed you in so many ways, but he isn't finished blessing you. There are still thousands of blessings God wants to shower upon you. One of the great blessings God wants to share with you is the Eucharist. Every day you are getting closer to receiving Jesus in the Eucharist! Are you excited?

The Eucharist is food for the soul. That's right, your soul gets hungry just like your body gets hungry. It's easy to tell when your body gets hungry because your tummy growls and you feel weak and tired. But how do you know when your soul is hungry? When our souls are hungry we become restless, impatient, angry, and selfish. But most of all, we find it harder to do what we know we should do.

When our souls get hungry we need to feed them. The Eucharist is the ultimate soul food, but we can also feed our souls with prayer, the Scriptures, and serving other people.

**My Notes:**

_____

_____

_____

_____

_____

_____

_____

You feed your body every day. You don't wait until it is starving before you feed it. You have a regular routine of meals and snacks to make sure your body has the food and energy it needs to thrive. We need a routine like that for feeding our souls too. This routine includes daily prayer, grace before meals, service to others, and of course, Sunday Mass.

The Mass is an incredible blessing because it feeds your soul in many ways. The Word of God feeds your soul, receiving the Body and Blood of Jesus in the Eucharist feeds your soul, and participating in a community of faith feeds your soul.

We've already talked about the Word of God and how important it is to listen to God. Now let's talk about how he feeds us with the Eucharist.

5 minutes

**tip**

The illustration depicts the Israelites gathering Manna in the desert. If time allows, tell the children about the image. God sent the Israelites food from heavenso they could survive theirjourney through the desert. It was a daily miracle worked by a God who loves his people. Everyday at Masses all over the world, God works an even more amazing miracle for us through the Eucharist.

**Jesus is the hungry one. I believe that God is hungrier for our love than we are for his love. He is hungrier to give his love than we are to receive.**

St Teresa of Calcutta

## WATCH AND DISCUSS

### Step-by-Step

**1** Introduce Episode 2 by saying: "Fr. Tom helps Ben, Sarah, Elijah, Tiny, Max, Isabella, and Jessica understand the Liturgy of the Eucharist."

**2** Watch Episode 2.

**We have a universal hunger for the authentic, a longing to be and become and experience all we are capable of and created for. Everything good in our future depends on whether or not we will follow this longing.**

Rediscover Catholicism

## The Liturgy of the Eucharist

You are so blessed to be Catholic. One of the many reasons you are blessed to be Catholic is the Eucharist. You get to receive the Body and Blood of Jesus. The Eucharist is uniquely Catholic.

You are Catholic. You are blessed.

The Liturgy of the Eucharist is broken up into three parts: the Offering, the Eucharistic Prayer, and the reception of Holy Communion.

This is all very important, so let's go over it together, step by step.

**My Notes:**

_____

_____

_____

_____

_____

_____

_____

_____

**8 minutes**

## tip

The children will learn not only from the words you say, but also by the manner in which you live. Take to heart the words of St. Paul to Titus: "In everything set them an example by doing what is good. In your teaching show integrity, seriousness and soundness of speech that cannot be condemned . . ." (Titus 2:7-8).

Did you learn something new about the Liturgy of the Eucharist watching the video or did something really strike you? If so, share this with the students!

_____
_____
_____
_____
_____
_____
_____

**The Eucharist is the secret of my day. It gives me strength and meaning to all my activities of service to the Church and the whole world.**

St. John Paul II

## READ AND EXPLORE

### Step-by-Step

**1** Read out loud the fifth and sixth paragraphs to the children.

**2** Ask the children to write in their books one way they would like to ask God to help in their lives this Sunday.

**Offer God everything. Mentally and spiritually place them all on the altar so that God can transform them.**

Rediscover Catholicism

## The Offertory

Throughout the Mass, God gives us moments to pause and experience its many wonders. The offertory is one of those moments.

During the offertory a family from the parish usually brings the bread and wine, along with the money we put in the collection for the Church and the poor. Then the priest prepares the gifts to offer them to God.

As the gifts are being brought forward and the priest is preparing the gifts, we offer ourselves completely to God. We can do this with a simple prayer in our hearts. Here is an example:

> Lord, I give myself completely to you right now. Teach me, lead me, and feed me with the Eucharist so I can serve you powerfully here in this world and live with you forever in heaven.

The offertory is also a great time to bring our problems to God and ask for his help. If there is someone you know who is suffering or something that you are struggling with, ask Jesus to heal the situation. He is the great healer. The offertory is a perfect time to ask Jesus the Healer to intervene in your life. Here are some examples:

> Jesus, help me study hard for my test.
> Jesus, my friend is sick. Help her to get better.
> Jesus, my brother hurt my feelings. Help me to forgive him.
> Jesus, help me to listen better to my parents.

**My Notes:**

_____

_____

_____

_____

_____

_____

_____

_____

You are on a great journey with God. Your destination is heaven. God wants to be your guide and companion on this journey. He wants to be invited into every detail of your life so that he can best guide and advise you. He wants to show you the best way to live. God wants to help you become the-best-version-of-yourself, grow in virtue, and live a holy life.

**5 minutes**

**tip**
Share an appropriate way you would like to ask God to help you in your life this Sunday.

**Give me your heart, my son, and let your eyes delight in my ways.**

Proverbs 23:26

**Step-by-Step**

**1** Ask the students: "What is the most important part of the Mass?"

- THE EUCHARISTIC PRAYER

**2** If time allows, ask a follow-up question: "Why is the Eucharistic prayer the most important part of the Mass?"

- BECAUSE THIS IS WHEN JESUS COMES TO BE WITH US.

## The Eucharistic Prayer

We've always celebrated the presence of God.

The Jewish people believed that God was present in the Ark of the Covenant. For a long time, the Ark was lost. This was a very sad time for the Jewish people. They tried very hard to find it because they wanted to be close to God.

When King David brought the Ark of the Covenant to Jerusalem, the people were overjoyed. So was King David. He was so happy that when he brought the Ark back to his people, he danced with great joy. Nothing made King David happier than being in the presence of God.

The Eucharist is God in our midst.

**The Eucharist is our family meal. It is the gift of God. Our worship focuses on the altar because that is how and where Jesus presents himself to us.**

Allen Hunt

**My Notes:**

_____

_____

_____

_____

_____

_____

_____

_____

Every time we go to Mass or visit a Catholic Church where Jesus is inside the tabernacle, God is physically with us in the Eucharist. The word Eucharist means "thanksgiving:" we are thankful to have God with us always.

The Eucharistic Prayer is the most important part of the Mass because this is when Jesus comes to be with us. This is when the bread and wine become the Body and Blood of Jesus.

During the Eucharistic Prayer we thank God for his friendship and for coming once again through the Eucharist to share his life with us.

**7 minutes**

**tip**

The Eucharistic prayer is the most important part of the Mass and it is the most important part of today's lesson. Jesus literally becomes physically present in the Eucharist. The bread and wine are transformed into the Body and Blood of Jesus. Don't move on from this illustration until every student in your class understand the importance of the Eucharistic prayer.

**David danced before the Lord with all his might.**

2 Samuel 6:14

119

## READ AND EXPLORE

**Step-by-Step**

**1** Invite the children to explore the illustration.

**2** Ask: "What scene in the Jesus story is this picture from?"

- JESUS' ENTRANCE INTO JERUSALEM THE WEEK HE IS KILLED. WE REMEMBER THIS MOMENT EVERY YEAR ON PALM SUNDAY.

**3** Tell the students: "As Jesus entered Jerusalem for the last time, the people laid palm branches down and shouted 'Hosanna! Blessed is the one who comes in the name of the Lord! Blessed is the coming of our ancestor David! Hosanna in the highest heaven!' (Mark 11:9–10). Sound familiar?"

## The way of God is one of peace and order.

Decision Point

## The Consecration

The consecration is the moment when the bread and wine become the Body and Blood of Jesus. This is an incredible moment—that's why we kneel down for the consecration. Kneeling is a simple and profound sign of reverence. When we kneel during the Mass, it is a sign that something amazing is about to happen.

Just before kneeling, we pray the *Holy, Holy, Holy* together as a parish family:

**My Notes:**

_____

_____

_____

_____

_____

_____

_____

**Holy, Holy, Holy Lord God of Hosts.**
**Heaven and earth are full of your glory.**
**Hosanna in the highest.**
**Blessed is he who comes in the name of the Lord.**
**Hosanna in the highest.**

Now we kneel and prepare for the great moment of consecration. Leading up to the consecration, the priest reminds us what happened at the Last Supper, the very first Eucharist.

To consecrate the bread and the wine, the priest says the same words Jesus said during the Last Supper:

**This is my Body, which is given up for you;**
**This is the Blood of the new and everlasting covenant,**
**do this in memory of me.**

8 minutes

**tip**

If time allows, share with the children why Hosanna is such a special word. At the end of his life, Jesus returned to Jerusalem for the last time. When he arrived, the crowds said, "Blessed is he comes in the name of the Lord! Hosanna in the highest!" (Matthew 21:9). The people used the word Hosanna because they wanted Jesus to save to save them. So when we use the word at Mass, we are recognizing that Jesus is the our savior.

**The more you stay away from Communion, the more your soul will become weak, and in the end you will become dangerously indifferent.**

St. John Bosco

121

## READ AND EXPLORE

**Step-by-Step**

**1** Activity: STRETCH! Have the children stand up and follow your directions for an easy and instant energizer. Reach for the ceiling, then touch the floor. Reach up and lean to the right, then to the left. If possible, play a song during this period of stretching. Play "Let it Shine" from *Blessed: A Collection of Songs for the Young at Heart.*

**These mysteries are mysteries, but if we approach them humbly, often, and with reverence, God will give us an ever-increasing love and understanding of them.**

Rediscover Catholicism

## Our Father

This is the moment of consecration. After the priest says these words, the bread and wine become the Body and Blood of Jesus. The consecration of the Eucharist is one of the great mysteries of our faith.

The Eucharistic Prayer ends with the Great Amen. Sometimes we say the Amen and sometimes we sing it. Either way we should say it loud and with confidence. This is our way of saying, "Yes! Jesus, I believe in you! I believe that the bread and the wine just became your Body and Blood!"

Following the Great Amen, we stand and pray the *Our Father* together.

**My Notes:**

_____

_____

_____

_____

_____

_____

_____

_____

Do you remember one of the main reasons why Jesus taught us this prayer? We talked about it while preparing for your First Reconciliation. Let's revisit it for a moment.

**You are blessed. You are the son or daughter of a great King. Jesus wanted us to always remember that God is our Father and that we are children of God.**

The *Our Father* reminds us of the first blessing God gives us: life!

After the *Our Father*, the priest asks God to fill us with his peace. Remember how earlier we talked about your soul getting hungry? One sign that your soul is hungry is that you don't have peace in your heart. Your soul craves peace.

God wants to fill you with his peace so that you can go out into the world and share it with everyone who crosses your path.

**5 minutes**

**tip**

Do you have a favorite prayer in the Mass? If you do, share it with the children. My favorite prayer comes right after the *Our Father* when the priest says, "Deliver us, Lord, from every evil and grant us peace in our days. In your mercy keep us free from sin, and protect us from all anxiety as we wait in joyful hope for the coming of our Savior, Jesus Christ."

_____

_____

_____

_____

_____

_____

**Acquire the spirit of peace and thousands around you will be saved.**

St. Seraphim of Sarov

123

## WATCH AND DISCUSS

### Step-by-Step

**1** Introduce Episode 3 by saying: "Fr. Tom, leads Ben, Sarah, Hemingway, and their friends on an adventure. Let's find out where they end up!"

**2** Watch Episode 3.

**3** Read John 3:16 on page 124 out loud to the children.

**4** Ask the students to turn to page 125. Point them to the last paragraph on that page. Ask the students to say it out loud together.

**5** Ask the children how it felt to say those words.

**Catholicism is a powerful humanizing force in our lives when we embrace it with humble hearts.**

The One Thing

# Holy Communion

When you receive Holy Communion Jesus gives himself completely to you. In the prayers leading up to the consecration we remember that Jesus died for us on the cross to save us from our sins. This is not meant to make you feel guilty; it is meant to make you feel loved. God wants you to remember how much you mean to him.

One of the most famous passages in the entire Bible is John 3:16:

> **For God so loved the world that he sent his only Son, so that everyone who believes in him may not perish but have eternal life.**

**My Notes:**

_____

_____

_____

_____

_____

_____

_____

God loved you so much that he sent his son, Jesus, so that you could have eternal life. For God so loved YOU that he sent Jesus so that YOU may have eternal life! You are loved and indeed blessed!

Let's say this out loud together:

**God loves me so much that he sent his son Jesus so that I could have eternal life and live with him forever in heaven.**

8 minutes

**tip**

The entire Gospel is captured in John 3:16. Take a moment to share how much God's love means to you.

**Worship the Lord with gladness; come before him with joyful songs.**

Psalm 100:2

## READ AND EXPLORE

### Step-by-Step

**1** Read the text out loud to the children.

**2** Ask the children if they have any questions about what it will be like to receive Jesus for the first time. Be prepared to share a memory from your First Communion to get the conversation started.

**The moment when I receive the Eucharist is a pivotal moment in my week. It's a moment of transformation, a moment where I get to receive who and what I wish to become.**

The One Thing

How did that feel?

God always wants you to feel loved. And when we receive Jesus in the Eucharist this is a special moment of God's love.

If you ever get to climb a huge mountain, the feeling of looking out across the vast surroundings from the top of that mountain is an amazing experience. The Mass is like climbing a great mountain. Receiving the Eucharist is the top of the mountain, the pinnacle of the Mass.

God feeds us the ultimate food for the soul at the mountaintop of the Mass. The Eucharist is food for the soul. Every Sunday at Mass God fills us with the Eucharist to become the-best-version-of-ourselves, grow in virtue, and live holy lives.

**My Notes:**

_____

_____

_____

_____

_____

_____

_____

Receiving Holy Communion is an incredible gift that we should never take for granted.

When the moment arrives to receive Jesus, you will stand before the priest, deacon, or extraordinary minister and he will raise the host and say, "The Body of Christ." You will respond by saying, "Amen," and then consume the Host.

**4 minutes**

**When you receive Holy Communion, close your bodily eyes so that you may open the eyes of your soul. Then look upon Jesus in the center of your heart.**

St. Teresa of Avila

127

**Step-by-Step**

**1** Introduce Episode 4 by saying: "Fr. Tom shares an amazing story about a miracle that took place in Italy. I can't wait for you to hear it!"

**2** Watch Episode 4.

**It is the belief that Jesus is truly present in the Eucharist—not just symbolically so— that seems to be one of the key differences between highly engaged Catholics and those who walk away from the Church.**

The One Thing

# The True Presence

Jesus is truly present in the Eucharist. It is not a symbol; it is Jesus. This is one of the most beautiful mysteries of the Catholic Faith.

When Jesus first started telling people about the Eucharist, some found it difficult to believe. Throughout the centuries, others have had doubts about Jesus being truly present in the Eucharist too.

In the 8th century there was a priest in Italy who was having these doubts. One day while he was saying Mass, as he consecrated the bread and wine they literally turned into living flesh and blood. It was an incredible miracle! The Church calls this a Eucharistic miracle.

Normally during Mass, we are unable to see the physical change from bread and wine to the Body and Blood of Christ. We have faith that the change takes place. But at this particular moment in time God decided to show the world what happens during every Mass.

Today, you can travel to Lanciano, Italy, where the miracle took place and see the flesh and the blood from that miracle over a thousand years ago.

Every time you go to Mass, the change from bread and wine to the Body and Blood of Jesus occurs. Jesus is truly present in the Eucharist. This is an incredible gift! You are blessed to be able to receive Jesus in the Eucharist.

**My Notes:**

_____

_____

_____

_____

_____

_____

_____

_____

4 minutes

**tip**

Share your own amazement that the Eucharist is not a symbol but really is the true presence of Jesus. Talk about your favorite part of the miracle at Lanciano. Don't shy away from sharing your personal feelings about the miracle. Your students will enjoy hearing your thoughts.

**I am the bread of life. Whoever comes to me will never be hungry, and whoever believes in me will never be thirsty.**

John 6:35

129

## WATCH AND DISCUSS

### Step-by-Step

**1** Introduce Episode 5 by saying: "Ben tells us about the moment the disciples received their First Communion."

**2** Watch Episode 5.

> To say we are bored at any moment in our lives is a massive insult to God, but to say we are bored at Mass takes the insult to a whole other level.

Resisting Happiness

## From the Bible: The Last Supper

On the night before he died Jesus gathered his disciples for one last meal together. It was the Jewish feast of Passover.

While they were together at the table Jesus spoke to them about how he was going to be betrayed and suffer.

Then while they were eating, Jesus took a loaf of bread, and after blessing it, he broke it and gave it to his disciples, saying, "Take this, all of you, and eat it; this is my Body." Then he took a cup, and after giving thanks, he gave it to them, saying, "Take this, all of you, and drink from it; this is the cup of my Blood, which will be poured out for many, for the forgiveness of sins."

When they had finished their meal, they went out to the Mount of Olives.

Adapted from Matthew 26:26–30

**My Notes:**

_____

_____

_____

_____

_____

_____

_____

This is known as the Last Supper, the most famous meal in the history of the world. At the Last Supper Jesus did something incredible. He turned ordinary bread and wine into his Body and Blood. The Last Supper was the first Eucharist, and the disciples' First Communion.

There in that room two thousand years ago, Jesus gave himself to the disciples. And every time we receive the Eucharist he gives himself to us in the same way!

Jesus wants to be invited into your life. He wants to be your friend. He wants to encourage you, guide you, listen to you, and love you. Jesus wants to help you become the-best-version-of-yourself, grow in virtue, and live a holy life. You are blessed!

3 minutes

_____
_____
_____
_____
_____
_____
_____

**tip**
If time allows, ask the children what the disciples felt during the Last Supper. Were they nervous, excited, confused, grateful, humbled, honored, happy?

**If we but paused for a moment to consider attentively what takes place in this Sacrament, I am sure that the thought of Christ's love for us would transform the coldness of our hearts into a fire of love and gratitude.**

St. Angela of Foligno

## WATCH AND DISCUSS

### Step-by-Step

**1** Introduce Episode 6 by saying: "In this episode, Ben and Sarah give us some great ideas on how we can share God's blessings with others!"

**2** Watch Episodes 6.

**To be one with God is a beautiful thing, and whether you are aware of it or not, it is your deepest yearning. You have an insatiable yearning to be one with God.**

Decision Point

## Jesus Is in You

After you receive Jesus in the Eucharist you will make your way back to your seat. At this moment, Jesus is in you. Amazing!

If Jesus came to visit you at your house, imagine how you would prepare for his arrival, imagine how excited you would be for him to get there, and imagine how you would sit by him and listen to everything he had to say.

Well, not only does Jesus come to visit us in the Mass, but he makes his home within us when we receive the Eucharist. So, when you get back to your seat after receiving Jesus in the Eucharist, this is a very special time of prayer.

Kneel or sit down, close your eyes, and talk to Jesus in your heart. This is a very special moment. Jesus is inside you. Thank him for all the ways he has blessed you. Count your blessings, one by one, with Jesus.

**My Notes:**

_____

_____

_____

_____

_____

_____

_____

_____

The Eucharist energizes and nourishes your soul. You receive many gifts each time you receive the Eucharist. This is a short list of some of those gifts:

Friendship with Jesus
Desire to do the will of God
Cleansing of venial sin
Hunger for virtue
Grace to avoid sin in the future
A heart that listens to the Holy Spirit
Desire to know and love God

Your First Communion is a very important moment in your life, but every time we receive Jesus in the Eucharist is an incredible gift that we should never take for granted.

🕐 5 minutes

**tip**

The moments after receiving Communion are special. If time allows encourage the children to spend the time after Communion thanking God for all the ways he has blessed them. Remind them that this is a very special time between them and Jesus.

**In an ever changing world the Holy Eucharist is a constant reminder of the great reality of God's changeless love.**

St. Teresa of Calcutta.

# READ AND EXPLORE

### Step-by-Step

**1** Read the last two paragraphs out loud to the children.

**2** Ask: "How can you share your blessings with others?"

- HELP A FRIEND WITH HOMEWORK.
- CLEAN MY ROOM.
- MAKE A THANK YOU CARD FOR MY PARENT OR GRANDPARENT.
- DO CHORES WITHOUT BEING ASKED.
- DONATE CLOTHES.

**In this final moment of the Mass we are being sent on a mission to light up the ways of this world with the love of Christ, a love that is willing to sacrifice for others, a love that has no limits.**

Rediscover Catholicism

134

My Notes:

_____

_____

_____

_____

_____

_____

_____

_____

# The Concluding Rites

After we have had a few quiet minutes of prayer with Jesus, it is time for the final prayer and blessing.

> **Priest: May Almighty God bless you, the Father, the Son, and the Holy Spirit.**
> **Congregation: Amen!**
> **Priest or Deacon: Go forth, the Mass is ended.**
> **Congregation: Thanks be to God!**

In the final blessing we are being sent forth. Sent to do what? God's work in the world. At the end of Mass, God sends you out on a mission. He has fed you with his Word and the Eucharist. He has provided you with everything you need to bring his love to the world you live in.

You are blessed and God wants you to go out into the world and share your blessings with others.

6 minutes

_____

_____

_____

_____

_____

_____

**tip**

The children are not too young to be thinking of ways they can share their blessings. They are the perfect age to begin godly habits! Great leaders cast a vision of who their students could be in order to help them become what they are capable of.

**You will receive power when the Holy Spirit comes on you; and you will be my witnesses in Jerusalem, and in all Judea and Samaria, and to the ends of the earth.**

Acts 1:8

## SHOW WHAT YOU KNOW

**Step-by-Step**

**1** Have your children complete the activity page by themselves, with a partner, or as a group.

**2** After three minutes ask the class, "Are there any questions you are struggling with?"

**3** Briefly explain the answer to any questions they might have, referring back to the specific page in the workbook.

**Building character is a task only for the brave and dedicated.**

The Rhythm of Life

## Show What You Know

**True or False**

1. __T__ One of the great blessings God wants to share with you is the Eucharist. (p 112)

2. __T__ The Eucharist is uniquely Catholic. (p 114)

3. __F__ The bread and wine don't become the Body and Blood of Jesus. (p 119)

4. __F__ Our souls are not nourished by the Eucharist. (p 112)

5. __T__ Jesus is truly present in the Eucharist. (p 128)

**Fill in the blank**

1. There are _____thousands_____ of blessings God wants to shower upon you. (p 112)

2. The _____Eucharist_____ is food for your soul. (p 126)

3. You are so blessed to be _____Catholic_____. (p 114)

4. Receiving Holy Communion is an incredible _____gift_____ that we should never take for granted. (p 127)

5. You are on a great _____journey_____ with God and your destination is _____heaven_____. (p 117)

**My Notes:**

_____

_____

_____

_____

_____

_____

_____

6. The consecration is the moment when the bread and wine become the _____**body**_____ and _____**blood**_____ of Jesus. (p 120)

7. To consecrate the bread and wine, the priest says the same words Jesus used during the _____**Last Supper**_____. (p 121)

8. God fills you with _____**peace**_____ so that you can go into the world and share it with everyone who crosses your path. (p 123)

9. God _____**loves**_____ you so much that he sent his son, Jesus, so that you could have eternal life! (p 125)

10. You are _____**blessed**_____ and God wants you to go out into the world and share your _____**blessings**_____ with others. (p 135)

### Word Bank

| | |
|---|---|
| CATHOLIC | HEAVEN |
| BODY | BLOOD |
| BLESSINGS | JOURNEY |
| LAST SUPPER | LOVES |
| THOUSANDS | EUCHARIST |
| PEACE | BLESSED |
| GIFT | |

**8 minutes**

_____
_____
_____
_____
_____
_____
_____

**tip**

If you are running short on time, you may choose to complete this section together as a class. Simply read each fill in the blank and true and false statement and invite your students to call out the answer. Once someone calls out the right answer, ask everyone to write it down in their workbook. If you are completely out of time, ask the children to complete the exercise for homework.

**The true way to advance in holy virtues is to persevere in a holy cheerfulness.**

St. Philip Neri

# JOURNAL WITH JESUS

### Step-by-Step

**1** Invite your children to write a letter to Jesus.

**2** Ask the children to remain silent during their journaling time.

**3** You may wish to play some quiet, reflective music to help create the right mood in the classroom and to encourage the students to remain quiet and focused on journaling with Jesus.

**Our best days are those when we stay connected with God throughout the day.**

Rediscover Jesus

**My Notes:**

_____

_____

_____

_____

_____

_____

_____

_____

## Journal with Jesus

Dear Jesus,

I know you will never leave me because . . .

_____

_____

_____

_____

_____

_____

_____

_____

**5 minutes**

_____

_____

_____

_____

_____

**tip**
Spend some time walking around the classroom as the children write. Let them know you are here to help if they need it. Your presence will be reassuring but it will also keep them focused on the task at hand.

When Jesus spoke again to the people, he said, "I am the light of the world. Whoever follows me will never walk in darkness, but will have the light of life.

John 8:12

## CLOSING PRAYER

### Step-by-Step

**1** Prepare the children to pray with Ben. Get them settled and quiet.

**2** Watch Episode 7.

**3** Ask the children: "What are some of the most important things you learned in this session?"

- JESUS IS TRULY PRESENT IN THE EUCHARIST.

- THE EUCHARIST IS FOOD FOR OUR SOULS.

- HOLY COMMUNION IS A LIFELONG BLESSING THAT WE SHOULD NEVER TAKE FOR GRANTED.

- I AM BLESSED TO BE CATHOLIC.

- THE EUCHARISTIC PRAYER IS THE MOST IMPORTANT PART OF THE MASS.

- GOD LOVES ME SO MUCH THAT HE SENT HIS ONLY SON TO SAVE ME.

- FIRST COMMUNION IS A VERY IMPORTANT MOMENT IN MY LIFE.

## Closing Prayer

There is so much to be discovered about the Mass. You could spend a lifetime going to Mass every single day, and at the end of your life still be surprised by the beautiful meaning behind everything we do and say at Mass.

Our God is a God of surprises. We can never put limits on what he is capable of or how his love can transform something ordinary, like bread and wine, into something truly extraordinary, like the Body and Blood of Jesus.

Lord, catch me off guard today.
Surprise me with some moment
of beauty or pain.
So that at least for the moment I may be
startled into seeing that you are here in all your splendor,
always and everywhere, barely hidden, beneath, beyond,
within this life I breathe.

Amen.

Frederick Buechner

**My Notes:**

_____

_____

_____

_____

_____

_____

_____

_____

5 minutes

**tip**

Acts 1:8 says: "You will receive power when the Holy Spirit comes on you; and you will be my witnesses in Jerusalem, and in all Judea and Samaria, and to the ends of the earth." With each class, you are fulfilling Jesus' commission by sharing the Gospel with your students. Never forget that Jesus holds up his end of the bargain too. The power of the Holy Spirit is with you. Do not be afraid to call upon this power again and again.

**Ask and it will be given to you; seek and you will find; knock and the door will be opened to you.**

Matthew 7:7

# 5

# Your First Communion

## QUICK SESSION OVERVIEW

Opening Prayer. . . . . . . . . . . . . . . . . . . . . . . . . . . . . . . . . . 5 min

Watch and Discuss; Read and Explore . . . . . . . . . . . . . 57 min

Show What You Know . . . . . . . . . . . . . . . . . . . . . . . . . . . 10 min

Journal with Jesus . . . . . . . . . . . . . . . . . . . . . . . . . . . . . . 10 min

Closing Prayer. . . . . . . . . . . . . . . . . . . . . . . . . . . . . . . . . . 8 min

## OBJECTIVES

- **TO PROCLAIM** that we are ready to say "yes" to God and receive their First Communion.

- **TO EXPLAIN** that the Eucharist will empower us to do great things for God.

- **TO TEACH** that we will always have an open invitation from God to share in the great celebration of the Mass.

- ## **Look ridiculous.**
- ## **Share your own story.**

## WELCOME

It might sound counterintuitive, but the more ridiculous you feel when teaching, the better the class is going. Being vulnerable enough to be animated while reading or sharing a picture of yourself at your First Communion might feel awkward or silly to you, but its impact on the children cannot be understated.

A bit of extra enthusiasm can help reassure children who might be nervous or doubting whether they are ready to make their First Communion. Enthusiasm gives them permission to enjoy the experience, ask questions and best of all, model your excitement.

Receiving First Communion is a BIG deal! This is their time to say YES to God. So tell them they are ready to say yes to God. They are ready to say no anything that does not help them become the-best-version-of-themselves. They are ready to walk with God, and they are ready to receive Jesus in the Eucharist.

We've talked about it before but it bears repeating—few things will be more impactful for the children than sharing your own story, especially in this session. The children don't just want to hear what the Church has to say about Holy Communion. They want to hear about your experience.

How have prayer and fasting impacted your experience of the Mass? What has the Eucharist empowered you to do? How do you feel about Jesus being inside you after Holy Communion?

Feeling ridiculous is a good thing. Be excited. Share your story. And incredible things will happen.

**Prayer
Icon**

**Read and
Explore**

**Watch and
Discuss**

**Show What
You Know**

**Journal
with Jesus**

**Time
Tracker**

# OPENING PRAYER

### Step-by-Step

**1** Take a moment to get the children quiet and settled down.

**2** Invite the children to get ready to pray by closing their eyes and taking a deep breath.

**3** Make the Sign of the Cross and pray the opening prayer slowly and reflectively.

**Prayer helps us to discover who we are and what we are here for.**

Decision Point

**My Notes:**

_____

_____

_____

_____

_____

_____

_____

_____

# 5

# Your First Communion

God, our loving Father,
thank you for all the ways you bless me.
Help me to be aware that every person,
place, and adventure I experience is an
opportunity to love you more.
Fill me with a desire to change and to grow,
and give me the grace to become
the-best-version-of-myself in
every moment of every day.

Amen.

**5 minutes**

**tip**

How close are the children to the day of their First Communion? Consider creating a countdown. Put the number on the board or have the children write it in their books: 22 days until my First Communion! Anticipation compounds excitement.

**And we know that in all things God works for the good of those who love him, who have been called according to his purpose.**

Romans 8:28

## WATCH AND DISCUSS

### Step-by-Step

**1** Introduce Episode 1 by saying: "Sarah has a special gift for Hemingway, let's find out what it is together!"

**2** Watch Episode 1.

> **The secret to lasting success is knowing where your gifts come from.**
>
> Mustard Seeds

## This Is a Special Day

Have you ever been excited to give someone a gift? Maybe it was at Christmas or perhaps it was for someone's birthday. When you're really excited to give someone a gift, it's hard to keep that gift a secret. It's even harder to wait until the day of celebration to give the gift. It might feel like you're about to burst because you're so excited!

This is how God the Father feels when he thinks about giving you Jesus in the Eucharist. He knows how special this gift is, and he can hardly wait to share it with you.

Your First Communion is a very special day. You are blessed!

**My Notes:**

_____

_____

_____

_____

_____

_____

_____

On the morning of your First Communion, before you get dressed, before you receive any gifts, before you even have breakfast, begin the day quietly with God in prayer. Let's practice together now:

**Loving Father, thank you for blessing me in so many ways. Jesus, I am looking forward to receiving you in the Eucharist for the very first time. Holy Spirit, help me to pay attention and make the most of this fabulous day.**

**Amen.**

This is a very special day. You will remember your First Communion for the rest of your life. You are blessed!

**5 minutes**

### tip

This episode contains a prayer lead by Ben. Do the children pray along with Ben and Sarah? If not, encourage them to do so. If they do, affirm their instincts. Feel free to pause the episode and ask everyone to pray along with Ben.

**Shout aloud and sing for joy, people of Zion, for great is the Holy One of Israel among you.**

Isaiah 12:6

## WATCH AND DISCUSS

### Step-by-Step

**1** Introduce Episode 2 by saying: "Let's watch as Ben, Sarah, Hemingway, and their friends ride their bikes over to Max's house."

**2** Watch Episode 2.

**Great thoughts are beautiful. Great actions are inspiring.**

Decision Point

## You're Growing Up

When you think about all the things you can do today that you could not do one, two, or three years ago, you realize that you are growing up quickly.

One of the most significant signs that you are growing up is your ability to take responsibility for your own actions.

You are able to follow directions. For example, when parents or teachers ask you to do something, you are able to understand what they are asking and do it.

You are able to control your impulses. For example, when your brother or sister does something to upset you, you are able to control your anger. And you are able to listen to and follow your conscience. For instance, if a friend asks you to do something that

**My Notes:**

_____

_____

_____

_____

_____

_____

_____

is wrong you will hear your conscience advising you not to do it—and you are able to say no to your friend.

The Church chooses this time in your life to share the Eucharist with you because you have reached the age of reason. When we reach the age of reason we are able to determine the difference between right and wrong and take responsibility for our actions.

You are ready to say yes to God. You are ready to say no to anything that does not help you become the-best-version-of-yourself. You are ready to walk with God, and you are ready to receive Jesus in the Eucharist.

5 minutes

**Moral principles do not depend on a majority vote. Wrong is wrong, even if everybody is wrong. Right is right, even if nobody is right.**

Venerable Fulton Sheen

## WATCH AND DISCUSS

**Step-by-Step**

**1** Introduce Episode 3 by saying: "Let's watch as Hemingway and Sarah help us to remember why preparation is so important!"

**2** Watch Episodes 3.

**To pray so as to grow and become more like Christ is the challenge of every Christian.**

Mustard Seeds

## Preparation Matters

When you were preparing for your First Reconciliation we talked about how important preparation is. We Catholics prepare for everything that is important.

Just as great athletes prepare every time they compete, Catholics prepare for the biggest moments in life. The great champions of our faith are the saints. They are all masters at preparation. The saints teach us how to prepare to receive Jesus in the Eucharist.

**My Notes:**

_____

_____

_____

_____

_____

_____

_____

_____

You are preparing for your First Communion, but it is important to prepare every time we receive Jesus in the Eucharist. We do this with prayer and fasting.

## Prayer

One of the best ways to prepare to receive Jesus is to pray. Prayer is a conversation with God. We all need a few minutes each day in a quiet place to sit and talk to him.

We continue our conversation with God throughout the day. When we see something amazing, we can say: "Wow, God, did you see that?" When we are afraid to do something that we know we should do, we can say: "God, please give me the courage to do this." And when something wonderful happens, we can say: "God, thank you for all the ways you bless me!"

Let's pray together right now, asking God to help us in the final preparations for our First Communion.

**Loving Father, thank you for all the wonderful ways you bless me every day. Please prepare my mind, heart, and soul to receive your son Jesus in the Eucharist. And help me to always remember that you want the very best for me. Amen.**

🕐
**5 minutes**

**tip**

Are you having fun? One of the keys to your effectiveness as a leader is your ability to serve the children with joy. Joy is at the heart of any service we perform for another person.

**Rejoice always, pray continually, give thanks in all circumstances; for this is God's will for you in Christ Jesus.**

1 Thessalonians 5:16–18

**Step-by-Step**

**1** Give the children an opportunity to explore the illustration. Encourage them to ask questions and think creatively.

- WHERE IS JESUS?
- WHY IS IN HE IN THE DESERT ALONE?

**2** Read the text together to find out!

- JESUS WENT INTO THE DESERT TO PREPARE FOR HIS MISSION BY FASTING AND PRAYING FOR FORTY DAYS.

**Prayer helps us to keep things in perspective.**

Decision Point

### Fasting

Another way we prepare to receive Jesus in the Eucharist is by abstaining from food for one hour before Mass. What does abstaining mean? It means going without. That's right, we don't eat or drink anything except water for one hour before Mass.

Fasting has played an important role in helping people grow spiritually for thousands of years. Our Jewish ancestors fasted to say sorry to God for their sins, to prepare for important events, and they fasted so they could see God's will more clearly. And Jesus went into the desert and fasted for forty days to prepare for his mission.

**My Notes:**

_____

_____

_____

_____

_____

_____

_____

When you are an adult, the Church will invite you to fast on certain days, like Ash Wednesday and Good Friday. Right now, the Church invites you to fast for one hour before Mass.

Fasting makes us more mindful of God's presence. It reminds us of how dependent we are on God and helps us to hear his voice more clearly. Fasting reminds us of our spiritual hunger. It helps us grow closer to God.

Receiving Jesus in the Eucharist is an awesome privilege. We prepare with prayer and fasting.

Prayer, fasting, and receiving Jesus in the Eucharist all help us to become more perfectly the person God created us to be, to grow in virtue, and to live holy lives.

**10 minutes**

**tip**

In his letter to the Galatians, St. Paul wrote, "and it is no longer I who live, but it's Christ who lives in me" (Galatians 2:20). Living out the faith in an authentic way causes people to want to be with you. Why? Because it will no longer be you living and teaching, but Christ living and teaching through you.

**When a man begins to fast, he straightaway yearns in his mind to enter into converse with God.**

St. Isaac the Syrian

151

## WATCH AND DISCUSS

### Step-by-Step

 **1** Introduce Episode 4 by saying: "Ben is unsure if God will help him to do great things in life. Let's watch as Ben and his dad have an incredible conversation about the power of the Eucharist."

**2** Watch Episode 4.

**3** Ask the children: "What amazing thing will God do through you?"

**God invites you to empty yourself so that he can fill you up. This is the adventure of salvation, and we make this journey by learning to love God, neighbor, self, and indeed, life.**

Rediscover Catholicism

## The Eucharist Empowers Us to Do Great Things

The Eucharist empowers us to do great things for God. For two thousand years Christians have been doing wonderful things.

The first Christians changed the world by showing everyone how to live in loving community. By setting aside selfishness and loving each other they became great witnesses to God's love and fulfilled Jesus' vision: "Everyone will know you are my disciples if you love one another" (John 13:35).

The Eucharist empowered the saints to do great things for God too. It inspired and empowered St. Ignatius of Loyola to create schools and universities.

St. Teresa of Calcutta used to sit before the Eucharist for an hour each day just talking to Jesus. It gave her the strength and courage to care for the poorest of the poor.

Jesus in the Eucharist gave St. Francis of Assisi the strength to rebuild the Church and the wisdom to help men, women, and children grow spiritually.

**My Notes:**

_____

_____

_____

_____

_____

_____

_____

St. Thérèse of Lisieux received power from the Eucharist to do little things every day with great love.

The Eucharist gave St. Thomas Aquinas the ability to write great books that helped people discover the genius of the Catholic faith.

God has been using the Eucharist to empower people to do great things for two thousand years. I am so excited to see what the Eucharist empowers you to do with your life.

**12 minutes**

**Very truly, I tell you, the one who believes in me will also do the works I do and in fact, will do greater works than these, because I am going to the Father.**

John 14:12

153

## WATCH AND DISCUSS

### Step-by-Step

**1** Introduce Episode 5 by saying: "Did you know that the disciples had a First Communion, just like you? Let's watch as Ben shares with us the moment the disciples received their First Communion."

**2** Watch Episode 5.

**3** Ask the children: "What do you think the disciples felt during the last supper?"

- NERVOUS, EXCITED, CONFUSED, GRATEFUL, HUMBLED, HONORED, HAPPY . . .

## All the answers are in the tabernacle.

Decision Point

# From the Bible: The Visitation

When Mary was pregnant with Jesus, she went to visit her cousin Elizabeth, who was pregnant with John the Baptist. As soon as Mary arrived at Elizabeth's house, baby John heard the voice of Mary and leapt with joy.

Elizabeth felt John dancing in her womb and the Holy Spirit helped her to say these now famous words: "Blessed are you among women, and blessed is the fruit of your womb! And why is this granted to me, that the mother of my Lord should come to me? For behold, when the voice of your greeting came to my ears, the babe in my womb leaped for joy" (Luke 1:42–44).

**My Notes:**

_____

_____

_____

_____

_____

_____

_____

Mary then stayed with Elizabeth for three months before returning home.

Jesus was in Mary's womb. That's why the baby John danced for joy. He was so excited to be in Jesus' presence.

When you go to church there is usually a little red light on next to the tabernacle. This light means that Jesus is in the tabernacle. Mary was the first tabernacle; Jesus was inside her.

After you receive the Eucharist, Jesus will be in you. This should bring you great joy.

With Jesus alive within us, we are each called to go out into the world as his ambassadors and disciples. You can do this by being kind and generous. You can do it by living a holy life. You can do it by encouraging people.

God is sending you on a mission to bring his love to the world.

10 minutes

_____
_____
_____
_____
_____
_____
_____

**And, Mary said,"Yes," at that moment he came to her heart. What happened then? She who was so small became great to let him live and love in her.**

St. Teresa of Calcutta

## WATCH AND DISCUSS

### Step-by-Step

 **1** Introduce Episode 6 by saying: "In this episode, Sarah shares with us some of the great advice she received in the days before and after receiving her First Communion."

**2** Watch Episode 6.

**You need to feed your soul in order to live a full and happy life.**

Decision Point

## Your First but Not Your Last

This is your first but not your last Communion. Every Sunday when you go to Mass you can receive Jesus in the Eucharist. And if you are fortunate enough to go during the week for any reason, you can receive the Eucharist more than once a week. In fact, there are some people who go to Mass every day.

I want to encourage you to receive the Eucharist as often as you can, because the Eucharist fills us with the wisdom and courage to become the-best-version-of-ourselves, to grow in virtue, and to live the fabulous holy lives God wants us to live.

Just as we need to feed the body to give it the nourishment and energy it needs, we need to feed the soul too. We feed the soul with prayer, reading the Bible, and of course with the Eucharist, the ultimate food for the soul.

**My Notes:**

_____

_____

_____

_____

_____

_____

_____

_____

The Eucharist is a great blessing. You are blessed.

For the rest of your life you will have an open invitation to God's great banquet. God is the most generous host who has ever lived. He will never stop inviting you to share in this great celebration and he will never run out of food to nourish your soul.

There may be times when you wander away from God. But God will never stop calling you. He will never stop searching for you. God will never stop encouraging you to become the-best-version-of-yourself, grow in virtue, and live a holy life.

You are blessed.

10 minutes

**tip**

Right now, it is part of your mission to help the children feel blessed to receive Holy Communion for the first time. Take a moment and remind them how excited you are for them to receive their First Communion! If you brought a picture of yourself during your First Communion (or one of your children or grandchildren), this would be a great time to share it with them.

**And he took bread, gave thanks and broke it, and gave it to them, saying, "This is my body, given for you; do this in remembrance of me."**

Luke 22:19

## SHOW WHAT YOU KNOW

### Step-by-Step

**1** Have your children complete the activity page by themselves, with a partner, or as a group.

**2** After three minutes ask the class: "Are there any questions you are struggling with?"

**3** Briefly explain the answer to any questions they might have, referring back to the specific page in the workbook.

**The best thing you can do is to become the-best-version-of-yourself, because it is doing with purpose.**

The Rhythm of Life

## Show What You Know

### True or False

1. __T__ Your First Communion is a very special day. (p 145)

2. __F__ You are not ready to walk with God, and you are not ready to receive Jesus in the Eucharist. (p 147)

3. __F__ Prayer doesn't help us prepare to receive Jesus in the Eucharist. (p 149)

4. __F__ Fasting makes us mindful of God's presence. (p 151)

5. __T__ For the rest of your life you will have an open invitation to God's great banquet. (p 157)

### Fill in the blank

1. God the Father is so _____excited_____ when he thinks about giving you Jesus in the Eucharist. (p 144)

2. The Church chooses this time in your life to share the _____Eucharist_____ with you because you have reached the age of reason. (p 147)

3. We _____prepare_____ for everything that is important. (p 148)

4. The great champions of our faith are the _____saints_____. (p 148)

5. Prayer is a _____conversation_____ with God. (p 149)

**My Notes:**

_____

_____

_____

_____

_____

_____

_____

_____

6. Fasting helps us to grow _____ **closer** _____ to God. (p 151)

7. The Eucharist fills us with the _____ **wisdom** _____ and _____ **courage** _____ to become the- best-version-of-ourselves, to grow in virtue, and to live a holy lives. (p 156)

8. The Eucharist empowers us to do _____ **great** _____ things for God. (p 152)

9. After you receive the Eucharist, _____ **Jesus** _____ will be in you. (p 155)

10. God is sending you on a _____ **mission** _____ to bring his love to the world. (p 155)

### Word Bank

| | | | | |
|---|---|---|---|---|
| GREAT | EUCHARIST | CONVERSATION | WISDOM | MISSION |
| JESUS | EXCITED | COURAGE | CLOSER | PREPARE | SAINTS |

**10 minutes**

**Choose life, so that you and your children may live and that you may love the Lord your God, listen to his voice, and hold fast to him.**

Deuteronomy 30:19–20

# JOURNAL WITH JESUS

### Step-by-Step

**1** Invite your children to write a letter to Jesus.

**2** Ask the children to remain silent during their journaling time.

**3** You may wish to play some quiet, reflective music to help create the right mood in the classroom and to encourage the students to remain quiet and focused on journaling with Jesus.

**Allow God to inspire you, to fill you with his power, because he wants to send you out to inspire others.**

Rediscover Jesus

**My Notes:**

_____
_____
_____
_____
_____
_____
_____
_____
_____

# Journal with Jesus

Dear Jesus,

I hope receiving you in the Eucharist inspires me to . . .

_____

_____

_____

_____

_____

_____

_____

_____

**10 minutes**

_____

_____

_____

_____

_____

**There is nothing so great as the Eucharist. If God had something more precious, he would have given it to us.**

St. John Vianney

## CLOSING PRAYER

### Step-by-Step

**1** Prepare the children to pray with Ben. Get them settled and quiet.

**2** Watch Episode 7.

**3** Ask the children: "What are some of the most important things you learned in this session?"

- I AM READY TO SAY "YES" TO GOD AND RECEIVE MY FIRST COMMUNION.
- THE EUCHARIST WILL EMPOWER ME TO DO GREAT THINGS FOR GOD.
- THIS IS MY FIRST BUT NOT MY LAST COMMUNION.
- MY FIRST COMMUNION IS A REALLY SPECIAL DAY!
- I CAN PREPARE FOR MASS THROUGH PRAYER AND FASTING.

## Closing Prayer

Throughout the Gospels we hear about Jesus performing incredible miracles. He made the lame walk and the blind see, fed the hungry, and even raised Lazarus from the dead.

Jesus has the power to transform everyone he comes into contact with. Sometimes that transformation comes in a single moment, but most of the time that transformation happens slowly over our lifetime.

If you stay close to Jesus in the Eucharist, the power of God will do incredible things in your life too. The Eucharist will open the eyes of your soul and cure it of selfishness and blindness, so you can love generously.

Let's pray together now:

> My Lord and my God,
> I firmly believe that you are present in the Eucharist.
> Take the blindness from my eyes,
> So that I can see all people and things as you see them.
> Take the deafness from my ears,
> So that I can hear your truth and follow it.
> Take the hardness from my heart,
> So that I can live and love generously.
> Give me the grace to receive
> the Eucharist with humility,
> So that you can transform me a little more each day
> into the person you created me to be.
>
> Amen.

**My Notes:**

_____

_____

_____

_____

_____

_____

_____

_____

8 minutes

He cried with a loud voice, "Lazarus, come out!" The dead man came out, his hands and feet bound with strips of cloth, and his face wrapped in a cloth. Jesus said to them, "Unbind him, and let him go."

John 11:43–44

163

# 6

# God's Family

## QUICK SESSION OVERVIEW

Opening Prayer. . . . . . . . . . . . . . . . . . . . . . . . . . . . . . . . . . 4 min

Watch and Discuss; Read and Explore . . . . . . . . . . . . . 66 min

Show What You Know . . . . . . . . . . . . . . . . . . . . . . . . . . . 7 min

Journal with Jesus . . . . . . . . . . . . . . . . . . . . . . . . . . . . . . 5 min

Closing Prayer. . . . . . . . . . . . . . . . . . . . . . . . . . . . . . . . . . 8 min

## OBJECTIVES

- **TO PROCLAIM** that we are all made for mission.

- **TO EXPLAIN** that the parish is our spiritual family.

- **TO TEACH** that God created each of us with a purpose.

- # A lifelong blessing.
- # The ultimate food for the soul.

## WELCOME

In the 29th chapter of the *Book of Proverbs*, the following words appear, "Where there is no vision, the people will perish." This is true in every area of life. In a country where there is no vision the people will perish. In a marriage where there is no vision, people will perish. In a business, a school, or a family where there is no vision, the people will perish.

The same is true for the children in your class. First Communion is not just about one day. It's about the rest of their lives. It's about a lifelong invitation to God's great banquet. And it's about seeing the Eucharist as a lifelong blessing.

In this last session of the preparation experience, your main task is to cast a vision for the future. God has an incredible dream for every single child in your class. The Eucharist is essential to discovering that dream and having the courage to live out it out.

**Prayer Icon**

**Read and Explore**

**Watch and Discuss**

**Show What You Know**

**Journal with Jesus**

**Time Tracker**

# OPENING PRAYER

### Step-by-Step

**1** Take a moment to get your children quiet and settled down.

**2** Invite the children to get ready to pray by closing their eyes and taking a deep breath.

**3** Wait for the students to get quiet. Don't rush it; reverence takes patience and practice. When they are ready, begin with the Sign of the Cross.

**Developing a dynamic prayer life requires perseverance more than anything else. Just keep showing up.**

Decision Point

**My Notes:**

_____

_____

_____

_____

_____

_____

_____

# 6
# God's Family

God, our loving Father,
thank you for all the ways you bless me.
Help me to be aware that every person,
place, and adventure I experience is an
opportunity to love you more.
Fill me with a desire to change and to grow,
and give me the grace to become
the-best-version-of-myself in
every moment of every day.

Amen.

**4 minutes**

**tip**
Tell the children you are excited to see them. Encourage them by saying: "Let's make this our best class yet!" Share with them that you will be praying for each of them on the day of their First Holy Communion. Share your hope for it to be a special day that they always remember and cherish.

**This is the confidence we have in approaching God: that if we ask anything according to his will, he hears us.**

1 John 5:14

## WATCH AND DISCUSS

### Step-by-Step

**1** Introduce Episode 1 by saying: "Sarah has a special message for each of us, let's find out what it is!"

**2** Watch Episode 1.

**3** Reiterate what Sarah said in the episode. Tell the children: "You were all made for mission and I can't wait to see what special plan God has in store for you!"

**The Catholic lifestyle, when it is authentically presented and embraced, promotes the integration of every aspect of our daily lives and every aspect of the human person.**

Rediscover Catholicism

# Made for Mission

Now that you have discovered the healing power of God's forgiveness and the life-changing power of the Eucharist, it's a good time to think about why God has blessed you in so many ways.

God has blessed you because he loves you. He has blessed you because he wants you to live a fabulous life here on earth and to live in heaven with him forever. And God has blessed you because he made you for mission.

God gives every single person a mission. It may take some time to work out exactly what mission God is calling you to, but you have already learned about the most important part of your mission: to bring God's love to everyone you meet.

You were made for mission. God didn't make you just to have fun. He didn't create you to waste your time on things that are superficial. God made you for mission.

**My Notes:**

_____

_____

_____

_____

_____

_____

_____

5 minutes

**Then Jesus said to Simon, "Do not be afraid; from now on you will be fishers of men. When they had brought their boats to shore, they left everything and followed him.**

Luke 5:11

## WATCH AND DISCUSS

### Step-by-Step

**1** Introduce Episode 2 by saying: "Sarah wakes Ben and Hemingway up from a nap to start a great adventure!"

**2** Watch Episode 2.

**3** Ask: "Sarah mentioned some reasons why it's great to be Catholic. Can you name any?"

- OUR PARISH FAMILY CARES FOR US.

- THERE IS A CHURCH IN ALMOST EVERY PLACE AROUND THE WORLD.

- THE CATHOLIC CHURCH IS THE GREATEST FORCE FOR GOOD IN THE WORLD.

- THE CHURCH FEEDS THE HUNGRY, GIVES SHELTER TO THE HOMELESS, CLOTHING FOR THE NAKED, AND CARES FOR THE SICK.

## Your Parish Family

Did you know you belong to the most famous family in the world? That's right. You are blessed to be a member of the Catholic Church, and the Catholic Church is the most famous family in the world.

In almost every place around the world you can find a Catholic Church. You experience the Church through your local parish. Your parish is made up of men, women, and children just like you, who are all trying to become the-best-version-of-themselves and live holy lives.

When you were a baby your family took care of you. They fed you, cleaned you, and made sure you had what you needed to grow healthy

**My Notes:**

_____

_____

_____

_____

_____

_____

_____

and strong. Your parish feeds your soul. Your parish makes sure you have what you need to grow spiritually. Your parish helped you prepare for your First Reconciliation and your First Communion, so that you can be ready for the great mission God dreamed for you.

Throughout your life, there are going to be moments of great joy and moments of disappointment, failure, and sadness. All these experiences are part of life. We all experience them. But our spiritual family, our parish, is there for us through it all to comfort and care for us.

10 minutes

**tip**

Take a moment to share with the children the number one reason why you feel blessed to be Catholic. Along with the reasons listed on the previous page, here are a few more:

- IT'S THE CHURCH CHRIST STARTED AND SENT THE HOLY SPIRIT TO GUIDE.
- JESUS IS TRULY PRESENT IN THE EUCHARIST.
- MASS IS THE SAME ALL OVER THE WORLD.

**The nation doesn't simply need what we have. It needs what we are.**

St. Teresia Benedicta

169

## READ AND EXPLORE

### Step-by-Step

**1** Activity: STRETCH!
Have the children stand up and follow your directions for an easy and instant energizer. Reach for the ceiling, then touch the floor. Reach up and lean to the right, then to the left. If possible, play a song during this period of stretching. Play "Let it Shine" from *Blessed: A Collection of Songs for the Young at Heart* if you have the CD.

**The Gospel liberates us from selfishness by inspiring us to be generous. Decide right now, here, today, to live a life of staggering generosity.**

Rediscover Jesus

You are blessed! The Catholic Church is the greatest force for good in the world. Every day your Catholic family feeds millions of people all around the world. Through your generosity and mine together, we are able to give housing to the homeless and clothing for those who have none and take care of sick people in every country around the world.

Do you know why the Catholic Church does all this?

We do it because we are all God's children. We are one big family. We have been given the mission to bring God's love to every person on earth. And families take care of one another. The Catholic Church is the biggest family in the world, and you are a part of it.

You are blessed to be Catholic.

**My Notes:**

_____

_____

_____

_____

_____

_____

_____

Your parish is blessed to have you. I am excited to see the ways you use your talents to serve your parish. You see, your parish needs you. Without you, there would be a big hole in your parish. Your parish is helping you become the-best-version-of-yourself, but it also needs you to help it become the-best-version-of-itself.

That's right. God needs every parish in the world to be the-best-version-of-itself so that together they can powerfully serve every single person on earth. That's a big mission, isn't it?

Before Jesus ascended into heaven he said to his disciples, "Go out into the world and share my love and my message with every person in every country" (Matthew 28:19). He gives this same mission to you and me today. He wants us to share his love and his message with the world.

**5 minutes**

**tip**

G.K. Chesterton once wrote, "All men can be criminals, if tempted. All men can be heroes, if inspired." This is the last session that you will be with these children. It may sound cheesy, but make it count. Seriously, tell the children you are excited to see how God will inspire them to become the person he created them to be. If they ever need encouragement or inspiration remind them that it can always be found in Scripture, Mass, and daily prayer.

**The Church is the traveler's inn where the wounded are healed.**

St. Augustine of Hippo

**Step-by-Step**

**1** Introduce Episode 3 by saying: "We all have special talents but Sr. Rosa tells us about our greatest talent as humans!"

**2** Watch Episode 3.

**God's vision of love is beautiful, selfless, and radical.**

Decision Point

## Go Make a Difference

Once upon a time, there was a boy who lived by the ocean. Every afternoon he would walk along the beach. One day he noticed that as the tide had gone out it had left hundreds of starfish stranded on the sand. He realized the starfish would die if they were left there, so he started to pick them up one by one and throw them back into the water.

As the boy got to the other end of the beach, an old man came walking from the other direction. He saw what the boy was doing and said, "What are you doing, boy? You'll never make a difference. Why don't you just enjoy your walk?"

The boy ignored the old man and continued to pick the starfish up, one at a time, and throw them back into the water. But as the old man got closer, he came up to the boy and said, "You're wasting your time, boy. There are hundreds of them, maybe thousands. And there will be more tomorrow. You'll never make a difference."

The boy smiled, reached down in the sand, picked up one more starfish from the sand, and threw it as far as he could out into the ocean. Then he turned to the old man and said, "I made a difference for that one!"

**My Notes:**

_____

_____

_____

_____

_____

_____

_____

_____

8 minutes

**tip**

Positive reinforcement is a great friend. It helps the children to know what you expect and that you are seeing their efforts. For example, "Wow, Kyle, great job paying attention during that episode!"

**My only ambition is to serve God and love our neighbor well, we must manifest our joy in the service we render to him and them.**

St. André Bessette

173

## READ AND EXPLORE

**Step-by-Step**

**1** Read the text out loud.

**2** Ask the children to share some ideas on how they can make a difference in the lives of those around them.

- LISTEN TO THEIR PARENTS.
- DO THEIR HOMEWORK.
- BE KIND TO THEIR CLASSMATES.

**Ordinary people like you and me can answer most prayers.**

Resisting Happiness

You may be a great football player or a fabulous singer, but your greatest talent is your ability to make a difference in other people's lives. You will be amazed how you can bring joy to others by using this talent.

As disciples of Jesus we should always be looking for ways to make a difference in other people's lives. This is one of the ways we live out the mission that God has given us to bring his love to the world.

Just like the old man in the story, there will be people who try to discourage you. But the Holy Spirit is constantly encouraging you, saying, "You can do it!" "You're amazing!" "You can make a difference!" "You've got what it takes!"

**My Notes:**

_____

_____

_____

_____

_____

_____

_____

There will be times when you cannot do everything. For example, there are millions of hungry people in the world. You cannot feed them all, but you might be able to help feed one. Don't let what you can't do interfere with what you can do. Do your little bit. If everyone does their own little bit, we will change the world.

Jesus has given himself to you in the Eucharist. Now Jesus is sending you out into the world on a mission. There is a song we sing at church sometimes that perfectly summarizes this mission. It is called "Go Make a Difference." Here are some of the lyrics:

> Go make a difference; we can make a difference
> Go make a difference in the world
> Go make a difference; you can make a difference
> Go make a difference in the world.

🕐 **7 minutes**

_____
_____
_____
_____
_____
_____
_____

**tip**

To help with participation, make a game out of it. Take this question and divide the group into teams. Let the children answer the questions as a team and see which team comes up with the most answers.

**Therefore go and make disciples of all nations, baptizing them in the name of the Father and of the Son and of the Holy Spirit, and teaching them to obey everything I have commanded you. And surely I am with you always, to the very end of the age.**

Matthew 28:19–20

### Step-by-Step

**1** Introduce Episode 4 by saying: "Sr. Rosa shares with Ben, Sarah, Hemingway, and their friends one of the most powerful things we can do in life."

**2** Watch Episode 4.

**Without prayer, life doesn't make sense.**

Decision Point

## The Power of Prayer

Another powerful way for us to make a difference is by praying for other people. Prayer is powerful. Prayer makes a difference.

Perhaps you hear about a tornado on the other side of the world that has destroyed homes and fields, and now the people are hungry and homeless. You cannot go there and help them, and you may have no money to send them. But you can always pray for them.

Each day our prayer should be a great adventure that takes us all around the world. The adventure of prayer may begin in your own home, praying for your family; then perhaps you pray for your grandparents in California, or New York, or Florida; then you pray for a friend who moved to a new city; then you pray for the pope, in Rome; then you pray for the hungry children in Africa, and the people who were hurt in an earthquake in China. Prayer is a chance to travel all around the world.

And our prayer is not even limited to this world. We also pray for the souls in purgatory. Imagine being in purgatory and having nobody to pray for you. That would be quite sad, so we should each take a moment every day to pray for the souls in purgatory.

Prayer is a powerful way to make a difference. We can and should pray for ourselves, thanking God for all the ways he has blessed us and asking him to give us what we need to fulfill the mission he has given us here on earth. And we can and should pray for other people every day of our lives.

You are blessed, and you can bless others by praying for them.

**My Notes:**

_____

_____

_____

_____

_____

_____

_____

_____

7 minutes

**tip**

You have a willing audience here so why not encourage a daily prayer life? This is an excellent time to reinforce the power of daily prayer. The children are at the perfect age to get this healthy habit in place. Discuss a good place to pray in the home. It could be in their bedroom or favorite chair. Have them close their eyes and visualize their special place to pray. If time allows, invite the children to share where they plan to pray.

**Very early in the morning, while it was still dark, Jesus got up, left the house, and went off to a solitary place, where he prayed.**

Mark 1:35

177

## WATCH AND DISCUSS

### Step-by-Step

**1** Introduce Episode 5 by saying: "Sr. Rosa and the children discuss what it must have been like for the disciples through Jesus' Crucifixion, death, and Resurrection."

**2** Watch Episode 5.

**3** Ask the children: "Listen to these words of Jesus from the last verse of the book of Matthew: 'And remember, I am with you always, to the end of the age.' How does it feel to know Jesus is always with you?"

- THANKFUL
- HAPPY
- LOVED

**We can only love because God has loved us first, and he has loved us incredibly.**

Decision Point

178

## From the Bible: I Will Be With You Always

On Good Friday when Jesus was hanging on the cross, the disciples were sad and confused. They had placed all their hope in Jesus and now he was dead.

The disciples loved Jesus. He had been their teacher and their friend. They'd had great expectations that he would be the one sent from God to save them, just like they had read about in the Scriptures. But now he was gone and they felt deserted and alone.

Imagine how long Friday night was for them. They probably couldn't sleep, thinking about everything that had happened, wondering what would happen next. They were probably afraid that the people who had killed Jesus might try to kill them too.

I wonder what they did on Saturday. I wonder what they thought and what they said to each other. That Friday and Saturday were the worst days of their lives.

**My Notes:**

_____

_____

_____

_____

_____

_____

_____

_____

But on Sunday morning everything changed. Jesus rose from the dead. He had told them he would, but maybe they didn't understand, or maybe they forgot, or maybe they didn't believe!

When Jesus rose from the dead and appeared to the disciples, you can imagine how amazed and excited they were.

Over the next forty days Jesus appeared to many people, to encourage them in their mission and remind them of his great love.

When it was time for Jesus to ascend into heaven, he had a very important message for us all. He said to the disciples, "I am going now to be with my Father in heaven, but wherever you are in this world, I will always be with you at your side."

Adapted from Matthew 28:20

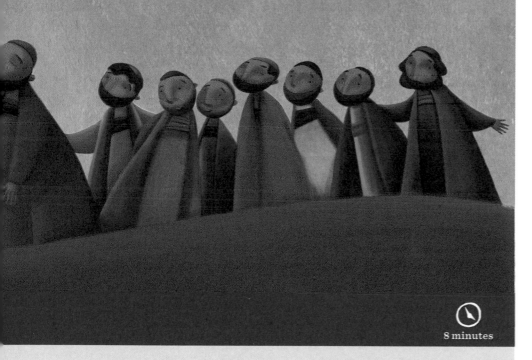

8 minutes

**tip**

Do you have a picture of your favorite image of Jesus? If so, share it with the children. Explain why this is your favorite image. Challenge them to look for their own favorite image of Jesus. Sacred art has always inspired the human heart.

**Remember that you are never alone, Christ is with you on your journey every day of your lives!**

St. John Paul II

### Step-by-Step

**1** Read the text out loud. Do your best to speak slowly and with great enthusiasm.

**2** Some things bear repeating! Reread the following: *Jesus wants you to remember that he is always there for you.*

Jesus has been keeping this promise for two thousand years. He is waiting for you to get out of bed when you wake up in the morning. He rides with you to school. He is there in class and on the playground. He cheers for you at soccer and baseball. And he tucks you into bed at night and kisses you on your forehead.

Jesus loves you and he wants to be with you.

He is also with us always in the Eucharist. Every time you visit a church and see that little red light on beside the tabernacle, Jesus is there with you in a very special way.

Life is difficult, and we often have to make big decisions. When I have to make a decision, I like to stop by church and sit with Jesus in the tabernacle and talk to him. I talk to him about the decision I need to make, and I ask him for his advice. Then I sit quietly and let him speak to my heart.

Jesus wants you to remember that he is always there for you. Whatever challenges come your way in life, you are never alone; Jesus is at your side. He is your friend and your teacher.

You are blessed!

**Hope is a good thing, maybe the best of things. Hope is one of those things you can't buy, but that will be freely given to you if you ask. Hope is the thing people cannot live without. Hope is a thing of beauty.**

Decision Point

**My Notes:**

_____

_____

_____

_____

_____

_____

_____

**5 minutes**

**tip**

Do you ever spend time before Jesus in the tabernacle? Do you consult Jesus before making a big decision in your life? If so, share that with the children.

**Pray with great confidence, with confidence based upon the goodness and infinite generosity of God and upon the promises of Jesus Christ.**

St. Louis de Montfort

181

## WATCH AND DISCUSS

### Step-by-Step

**1** Introduce Episode 6 by saying: "Ben, Sarah, and their friends have one last message for us. Let's watch together!"

**2** Watch Episode 6.

**Once you know the purpose of life, everything falls into place.**

Mustard Seeds

## Trusting God

Our God is a God of purpose. He does things on purpose and he made you for a purpose.

As you journey through life, look for the purpose in things. Eating is fun and pleasurable, but the purpose of food is to fuel the body. Going to school and seeing your friends is great, but the purpose of school is to learn new things. Winning at soccer is exciting, but the purpose of sports is to help us grow strong and stay healthy.

By realizing that God has a purpose for everything, we learn to trust him and the beautiful plans he has for our lives. Keep your eye on the purpose of things. If you are ever confused, ask God, "What is the purpose of . . . ?"

**My Notes:**

_____

_____

_____

_____

_____

_____

_____

_____

**tip**

Use your voice like an instrument. Vary the volume, speed, and excitement.

The Bible tells us that there is a time for everything. There is a time to laugh and a time to cry, a time to sow and a time to reap, a time to be born and a time to die, a time to rejoice and a time to mourn, a time to speak and a time to listen. And it is always a good time to trust in God and the beautiful plans he has for your life (Ecclesiastes 3:1).

This is a time for you to celebrate. Your First Communion is one of the great moments in your life. The Eucharist will help you become the-best-version-of-yourself, grow in virtue, and live a holy life.

**7 minutes**

**You can make many plans, but the Lord's purpose will prevail.**

Proverbs 19:21

## READ AND EXPLORE

**Step-by-Step**

**1** Read the text out loud.

**2** Share a personal sentiment of gratitude toward the children for the time you have spent together.

**3** Practice saying the prayer together: "Jesus I trust in you."

There may be times in your life when you feel like God is far away, but he is not. There may be times in your life when you feel that God has forgotten you, but he will never forget you. He is with you always, at your side.

Life is a wonderful journey. Anytime you feel lost or confused, turn to Jesus and ask him to guide you and comfort you. The Eucharist reminds us that God is with us and that he wants to take care of us.

There is a time for everything and a purpose for everything. Place your trust in God. Throughout the day, a very simple prayer to repeat is: Jesus, I trust in you.

**My Notes:**

_____

_____

_____

_____

_____

_____

_____

_____

## Lord, I trust in your plans. Please show them to me!

Mustard Seeds

tip

Make a plan to continue to pray for the children in your class. Let them know that, even though your time together is ending, you will continue to pray for them during their life's journey. Finish by sharing how proud you are of the students and how well they have prepared for their First Communion. Public affirmation is powerful.

Pray it over and over and over again. "Jesus, I trust in you. Jesus, I trust in you. Jesus, I trust in you."

It has been a pleasure joining you for this part of your journey. Everyone at Dynamic Catholic is praying for you every day. We hope the lessons you have learned preparing for your First Reconciliation and your First Communion will live with you forever.

You are blessed. Blessed to be Catholic, blessed to be alive, and blessed to be loved. Try to remind yourself of that each day. Each morning when you wake up, and each night when you go to bed, whisper quietly to yourself, "I am blessed."

**5 minutes**

**Those who know your name trust in you, for you, Lord, have never forsaken those who seek you.**

Psalm 9:10

185

# Show What You Know

## True or False

1. _____ God has blessed you because he loves you.

2. _____ Your parish doesn't need you to spread God's love.

3. _____ Prayer is a powerful way to make a difference.

4. _____ Jesus asks us to face life's journey alone.

5. _____ You are blessed.

## Fill in the blank

1. God made you for _____.

2. The Catholic Church is the greatest force for _____ in the world.

3. Our mission is to bring God's _____ to every person on earth.

4. Your _____ is your spiritual family.

5. Your greatest talent is your ability to make a _____ in other people's lives.

6. God has a _____ for everything.

7. _____ is a powerful way to make a difference.

8. The _____ will help you become the-best-version-of-yourself, grow in virtue, and live a holy life.

9. Anytime you feel lost or confused, turn to _____ and ask him to guide you and comfort you.

10. You are Catholic, you are alive, you are loved, and you are _____!

**Word Bank**

| | | | | |
|---|---|---|---|---|
| PRAYER | PARISH | EUCHARIST | MISSION | BLESSED |
| GOOD | JESUS | LOVE | PURPOSE | DIFFERENCE |

# JOURNAL WITH JESUS

### Step-by-Step

**1** Invite your children to write a letter to Jesus.

**2** Ask the children to remain silent during their journaling time.

**3** You may wish to play some quiet, reflective music to help create the right mood in the classroom and to encourage the students to remain quiet and focused on journaling with Jesus.

**It is only by placing God at the center of everything that we can make sense of life.**

Resisting Happiness

**My Notes:**

## Journal with Jesus

Dear Jesus,

I want to spread your love because . . .

_____

_____

_____

_____

_____

_____

_____

_____

**5 minutes**

_____

_____

_____

_____

_____

_____

_____

**Trust in the Lord with all your heart and lean not on your own understanding; in all your ways submit to him, and he will make your paths straight.**

Proverbs 3:5–6

# CLOSING PRAYER

## Step-by-Step

**1** Prepare the children to pray with Ben. Get them settled and quiet.

**2** Watch Episode 7.

**3** Ask the children: "What are some of the most important things you learned in this session?"

- I WAS MADE FOR MISSION.

- MY PARISH IS MY SPIRITUAL FAMILY.

- GOD CREATED ME FOR A PURPOSE.

- I AM BLESSED.

- MY GREATEST TALENT IS TO MAKE A DIFFERENCE IN OTHERS LIVES.

- PRAYER IS POWERFUL AND IT MAKES A DIFFERENCE IN OTHERS LIVES.

- GOD WILL NEVER LEAVE ME.

## Closing Prayer

Explorers carry compasses so they don't get lost. A compass is a tool with a little arrow on it that always points North. Even if you have no idea where you are, your compass will help you find your way home.

Life is a great journey. You are an explorer and Jesus is your compass. There will be times when you don't know what to do next. Turn to Jesus during those times; he wants to help you live an amazing life.

And remember, you are not the first one to make this great journey, and you are not alone. Just as you are praying for other people, there are some great people praying for you. The angels and saints are in heaven cheering for you and praying for you. Every time you make a decision, they are praying you make a great choice and, with God's help, become the-best-version-of-yourself.

So, let's pray with the angels and saints to finish our time together:

**My Notes:**

_____

_____

_____

_____

_____

_____

_____

Loving Father, thank you for all the ways you bless me.
Inspire me to share your love
with everyone who crosses my path.
Never let me forget that you are always with me.

Holy Mary, Mother of God, pray for us.
Saint Michael, the Archangel, pray for us.
Saint John the Baptist, pray for us.
Saint Joseph, pray for us.
Saint Peter, pray for us.
Saint Paul, pray for us.
Saint Matthew, pray for us.
Saint Mary Magdalene, pray for us.
Saint Anthony, pray for us.
Saint Francis, pray for us.
Saint Clare, pray for us.
Saint Catherine, pray for us.
All holy men and women of God, pray for us.

Amen.

8 minutes

**tip**

Thank the children for allowing you to journey with them as they prepared for their First Communion. Remind them that you will continue to pray for them. And encourage them to never forget that they are blessed!

**You cannot be half a saint; you must be a whole saint or no saint at all.**

St. Thérèse of Lisieux

# My Little Catechism

Your fabulous journey with God is just beginning. Along the way you will have many questions. Questions are good. God places questions in your heart and mind for many different reasons. Follow your questions, wherever they might lead you.

Some of your questions will be easy to find answers to. To help us answer many of our questions, our spiritual leaders have given us the Catechism of the Catholic Church. The answers we find there have been revealed by God and by nature over the centuries.

In the pages that follow we will share with you some questions you may have about God and life. The answers are easy to read but often hard to live. But the answers will help you become the-best-version-of-yourself, grow in virtue, and live a holy life.

There will be other times in your life when you have questions that cannot be answered by words on a page, for example what Vocation you are called to or what career you should pursue. At these times you will seek deeply personal answers to deeply personal questions.

These questions require a lot more patience. Seek the advice of wise people who love the Lord. Read what wise men and women before you have had to say on such topics. But, most of all, pray and ask God to show you his way.

As you make this journey you will encounter others who have questions. Help them as best you can to find the answers. People deserve answers to their questions.

And never, ever, forget . . . you are blessed!

1. **Q: Who made you?**

   A: God made you.

   > In the Bible: Genesis 1:1, 26–27; Genesis 2:7, 21–22
   > In the Catechism: CCC 355

2. **Q: Does God love you?**

   A: Yes. God loves you more than anyone in the world,
   and more than you could ever imagine.

   > In the Bible: John 3:16
   > In the Catechism: CCC 457, 458

3. **Q: Why did God make you?**

   A: God made you to know him, love him, to carry out the mission he entrusts to
   you in this world, and to be happy with Him forever in Heaven.

   > In the Bible: Deuteronomy 10:12–15; John 17:3
   > In the Catechism: CCC 1, 358

4. **Q: What is God?**

   A: God is an infinite and perfect spirit.

   > In the Bible: Exodus 3:6; Isaiah 44:6; 1 John 4:8, 16
   > In the Catechism: CCC 198–200, 212, 221

5. **Q: Did God have a beginning?**

   A: No. God has no beginning. He always was and he always will be.

   > In the Bible: Psalm 90:2; Revelation 1:8
   > In the Catechism: CCC 202

6. **Q: Where is God?**

   A: Everywhere

   > In the Bible: Psalm 139
   > In the Catechism: CCC 1

7. **Q: Does God see us?**

   A: God sees us and watches over us.

   > In the Bible: Wisdom 11:24–26; Jeremiah 1:5
   > In the Catechism: CCC 37, 301, 302

8.  **Q: Does God know everything?**

    A: Yes. God knows all things, even our most secret thoughts, words, and actions.

    In the Bible: Job 21:22; Psalm 33:13–15; Psalm 147:4–5
    In the Catechism: CCC 208

9.  **Q: Is God all loving, just, holy, and merciful?**

    A: Yes, God is loving, all just, all holy, and all merciful—and he invites us to be loving, just, holy, and merciful too.

    In the Bible: John 13:34; 1 John 4:8; Ephesians 2:4
    In the Catechism: CCC 214, 211, 208

10. **Q: Is there only one God?**

    A: Yes, there is only one God.

    In the Bible: Isaiah 44:6; John 8:58
    In the Catechism: CCC 253

11. **Q: Why is there only one God?**

    A: There can only be one God, because God, being supreme and infinite, cannot have an equal.

    In the Bible: Mark 12:29–30
    In the Catechism: CCC 202

12. **Q: How many Persons are there in God?**

    A: In God there are three Divine Persons, unique and distinct and yet equal in all things—the Father, the Son, and the Holy Spirit.

    In the Bible: 1 Corinthians 12:4–6; 2 Corinthians 13:13; Ephesians 4:4–6
    In the Catechism: CCC 252, 254, 255

13. **Q: Is the Father God?**

    A: Yes.

    In the Bible: Exodus 3:6; Exodus 4:22
    In the Catechism: CCC 253, 262

14. **Q: Is the Son God?**

    A: Yes.

    In the Bible: John 8:58; John 10:30
    In the Catechism: CCC 253, 262

15. **Q: Is the Holy Spirit God?**

A: Yes.

In the Bible: John 14:26; John 15:26
In the Catechism: CCC 253, 263

16. **Q: What is the Holy Trinity?**

A: The Holy Trinity is one God in three divine persons—Father, Son, and Holy Spirit.

In the Bible: Matthew 28:19
In the Catechism CCC 249, 251

17. **Q. What is free will?**

A: Free will is an incredible gift from God that allows us to make our own decisions. This incredible gift comes with incredible responsibility.

In the Bible: Sirach 15:14—15
In the Catechism: CCC 1731

18. **Q. What is sin?**

A: Sin is any willful thought, word, deed, or omission contrary to the law of God.

In the Bible: Genesis 3:5; Exodus 20:1—17
In the Catechism: CCC 1850

19. **Q: How many kinds of sin are there?**

A: There are two actual kinds of sin—venial and mortal.

In the Bible: 1 John 5:16—17
In the Catechism: CCC 1855

20. **Q: What is a venial sin?**

A: Venial is a slight offense against God.

In the Bible: Matthew 5:19; Matthew 12:32; 1 John 5:16—18
In the Catechism: CCC 1855, 1863

21. **Q: What is a mortal sin?**

A: Mortal sin is a grievous offense against God and his law.

In the Bible: Matthew 12:32; 1 John 5:16—18
In the Catechism: CCC 1855, 1857

22. **Q: Does God abandon us when we sin?**

A: Never. God is always calling to us, pleading with us, to return to him and his ways.

> In the Bible: Psalm 103: 9–10, 13; Jeremiah 3:22; Matthew 28:20; Luke 15:11-32
> In the Catechism: CCC 27, 55, 982

23. **Q: Which Person of the Holy Trinity became man?**

A: The Second Person, God the Son, became man without giving up his divine nature.

> In the Bible: 1 John 4:2
> In the Catechism: CCC 423,464

24. **Q: What name was given to the Second Person of the Holy Trinity when he became man?**

A: Jesus.

> In the Bible: Luke 1:31; Matthew 1:21
> In the Catechism: CCC 430

25. **Q: When the Son became man, did he have a human mother?**

A: Yes.

> In the Bible: Luke 1:26–27
> In the Catechism: CCC 488, 490, 495

26. **Q: Who was Jesus' mother?**

A: The Blessed Virgin Mary.

> In the Bible: Luke 1:30, 31; Matthew 1:21–23
> In the Catechism: CCC 488, 495

27. **Q: Why do we honor Mary?**

A: Because she is the mother of Jesus and our mother too.

> In the Bible: Luke 1:48; John 19:27
> In the Catechism: CCC 971

28. **Q: Who was Jesus' real father?**

A: God the Father.

> In the Bible: Luke 1:35; John 17:1
> In the Catechism CCC 422, 426, 442

29. Q: Who was Jesus' foster father?

A: Joseph.

> In the Bible: Matthew 1:19, 20; Matthew 2:13, 19—21
> In the Catechism: CCC 437, 488, 1655

30. Q: Is Jesus God, or is he man, or is he both God and man?

A: Jesus is both God and man; as the Second Person of the Holy Trinity, he is God; and since he took on a human nature from his mother Mary, he is man.

> In the Bible: Philippians 2: 6-7; John 1:14, 16; John 13:3; 1 John 4:2
> In the Catechism: CCC 464, 469

31. Q: Was Jesus also a man?

A: Yes, Jesus was fully God and fully human.

> In the Bible: Luke 24:39; 1 John 4:2—3
> In the Catechism: CCC 464, 469, 470

32. Q: On what day was Jesus born?

A: Jesus was born on Christmas day in a stable in Bethlehem.

> In the Bible: Luke 2:1—20; Matthew 1:18—25
> In the Catechism: CCC 437, 563

33. Q: What is the Incarnation?

A: The Incarnation is the belief that Jesus became man.

> In the Bible: John 1:14; 1 John 4:2
> In the Catechism: CCC 461, 463

34. Q: Did Jesus love life?

A: Yes.

> In the Bible: John 10:10; John 2:1—12
> In the Catechism: CCC 221, 257, 989

35. Q: If Jesus loved life why did he willingly die on the cross?

A: He died on the cross because he loved you and me even more than life.

> In the Bible: Romans 5:8; John 15:13; Ephesians 5:2
> In the Catechism: CCC 1825, 604

36. **Q: Why did Jesus suffer and die?**

A: So that we could be forgiven our sins, and live with him in heaven forever after this life.

In the Bible: John 3:16; 2 Corinthians 5:14–16
In the Catechism: CCC 604, 618, 620

37. **Q: What do we call the mystery of God becoming man?**

A: The mystery of the Incarnation.

In the Bible: John 1:14; 1 John 4:2
In the Catechism: CCC 461, 463

38. **Q: On what day did Jesus die on the cross?**

A: Good Friday, the day after the Last Supper.

In the Bible: John 19:16–40; Matthew 27:33–50
In the Catechism CCC 641

39. **Q: On what day did Jesus rise from the dead?**

A: On Easter Sunday, three days after Good Friday.

In the Bible: Matthew 28:1–6; Mark 16:1–8
In the Catechism: CCC 1169, 1170

40. **Q: What gifts do we receive as a result of being saved by Jesus?**

A: By dying on the cross Jesus restored our relationship with God and opened a floodgate of grace.

In the Bible: Luke 23:44–46; Romans 3:21–26; 2 Corinthians 5:17–21
In the Catechism: CCC 1026, 1047

41. **Q: What is grace?**

A: Grace is the help God gives us to respond generously to his call, to do what is good and right, grow in virtue, and live holy lives.

In the Bible: John 1:12–18; 2 Corinthians 12:9
In the Catechism: CCC 1996

42. **Q: What is Faith?**

A: Faith is a gift from God. It is a supernatural virtue that allows us to firmly believe all the truth that God has revealed to us.

In the Bible: Hebrews 11:1
In the Catechism: CCC 1814

43. **Q: What is Hope?**

A: Hope is a gift from God. It is a supernatural virtue that allows us to firmly trust that God will keep all his promises and lead us to heaven.

In the Bible: Romans 8:24—25; 1 Timothy 4:10; 1 Timothy 1:1; Hebrews 6:18—20
In the Catechism: CCC 1817, 1820—1821

44. **Q: What is Charity?**

A: Charity is a gift from God. It is a supernatural virtue that allows us to love God above everything else, and our neighbor as ourselves.

In the Bible: John 13:34; 1 Corinthians 13:4—13
In the Catechism: CCC 1822, 1823, 1825

45. **Q: Will God give you the gifts of Faith, Hope, and Charity?**

A: Yes, God gives the gifts of Faith, Hope, and Charity, freely to all those who ask for them sincerely and consistently.

In the Bible: 1 Corinthians 13:13
In the Catechism: 1813

46. **Q: How long will God love me for?**

A: God will love you forever.

In the Bible: John 13:1; Romans 8:35—39
In the Catechism: CCC 219

47. **Q: When did Jesus ascend into heaven?**

A: On Ascension Thursday, forty days after Easter.

In the Bible: Acts 1:9; Mark 16:19
In the Catechism: CCC 659

48. **Q: When did the Holy Spirit descend upon the Apostles?**

A: On Pentecost Sunday, fifty days after Easter.

In the Bible: John 20:21—22; Matthew 28:19
In the Catechism: CCC 731, 1302

49. **Q: What is meant by the Redemption?**

A: Redemption means that Jesus' Incarnation, life, death, and Resurrection paid the price for our sins, opened the gates of heaven, and freed us from slavery to sin and death.

In the Bible: Ephesians 1:7; Romans 4:25
In the Catechism CCC 517, 606, 613

50. **Q: What did Jesus establish to continue his mission of Redemption?**

A: He established the Catholic Church.

> In the Bible: Matthew 16:18
> In the Catechism: CCC 773, 778, 817, 822

51. **Q: Why do we believe that the Catholic Church is the one true Church?**

A: Because it is the only Church established by Jesus.

> In the Bible: Matthew 16:18
> In the Catechism: CCC 750

52. **Q: Does it matter to which Church or religion you belong?**

A: Yes, in order to be faithful to Jesus, it is necessary to remain in the Church he established.

> In the Bible: Mark 16:16; John 3:5
> In the Catechism: CCC 846

53. **Q: What are the Four Marks of the Church?**

A: One, Holy, Catholic, and Apostolic.

> In the Bible: Ephesians 2:20, 4:3, 5:26; Matthew 28:19; Revelation 21:14;
> In the Catechism: CCC 813, 823, 830, 857

54. **Q: How does the Church preserve the teachings of Jesus?**

A: Through Sacred Scripture and Sacred Tradition.

> In the Bible: 2 Timothy 2:2; 2 Thessalonians 2:15
> In the Catechism: CCC 78, 81, 82

55. **Q: How does the Church's calendar differ from the secular calendar?**

A: The first day of the Church's year is the first Sunday of Advent, not January 1st. The Church's calendar revolves around the life, death, and Resurrection of Jesus. Throughout the course of the Church's year the whole mystery of Jesus Christ is unfolded.

> In the Bible: Luke 2:1–20; 1 Corinthians 15:3–4
> In the Catechism: CCC 1163; 1171, 1194

**Going Deeper**

Over the course of the year, through the readings at Mass, the feast days and holy days, we experience the story of Jesus. The Church's calendar does this to remind us that Jesus' story is not just about what happened over two thousand years ago. It is about our friendship with him today. The mystery of his life, teachings, and saving grace are unfolding in your life and the life of the Church today.

56. Q: Did Jesus give special authority to one of the Apostles?

A: Yes, to Peter when Jesus said to him, "I will give you the keys of the kingdom of heaven, and whatever you bind on earth shall be bound in heaven, and whatever you loose on earth shall be loosed in heaven."

In the Bible: Mark 3:16, 9:2; Luke 24:34
In the Catechism: CCC 552, 881

57. Q: Who speaks with the authority that Jesus gave to St. Peter?

A: The pope who is St. Peter's successor, the Bishop of Rome, and the Vicar of Christ on earth.

In the Bible: Matthew 16:18; John 21:15–17
In the Catechism: CCC 891

58. Q: What is the name of the present pope?

A: Pope Francis.

In the Bible: Matthew 16:18; John 21:15–17
In the Catechism: CCC 936

59. Q: What is the sacred liturgy?

A: The Church's public worship of God.

In the Bible: John 4:23–24
In the Catechism: CCC 1069, 1070

60. Q: What attitude should we have when we participate in the sacred liturgy?

A: We should have the attitude of reverence in our hearts and respect in our actions and appearance.

In the Bible: Hebrews 12:28
In the Catechism: CCC 2097

61. Q: What is a Sacrament?

A: A Sacrament is an outward sign, instituted by Christ and entrusted to the Church to give grace. Grace bears fruit in those who receive them with the required dispositions.

In the Bible: 2 Peter 1:4
In the Catechism: CCC 1131

**Going Deeper**

God gives you grace to help you do what is good and right. When you are open to God, he also gives you the grace to be kind, generous, courageous, and compassionate toward others. Grace bears good fruit in our lives. One of the most powerful ways God shares his grace with us is through the Sacraments. This grace helps us to become the-very-best-version-of-ourselves, grow in virtue, and live holy lives.

62. **Q: How does Jesus share his life with us?**

A: During his earthly life, Jesus shared his life with others through his words and actions; now he shares the very same life with us through the Sacraments.

In the Bible: John 3:16; John 6:5–7
In the Catechism: CCC 521; 1131, 1115–1116

**Going Deeper**

God loves to share his life and love with us. We can experience his life through daily prayer, Scripture, and through serving one another. The most powerful way that God shares his life with us is through the Sacraments. Sunday Mass and regular Reconciliation are two Sacraments that guide us and encourage us on our journey to become the-best-version-of-ourselves, grow in virtue, and live holy lives.

63. **Q: How many Sacraments are there?**

A: Seven.

In the Bible: John 20:22–23; Luke 22:14–20; John 7:37–39; James 5:14–16; Hebrews 5:1–6; Matthew 19:6
In the Catechism: CCC 1113

64. **Q: What are the Seven Sacraments; and which ones have you received?**

A: Baptism, Penance, Holy Eucharist, Confirmation, Holy Orders, Matrimony, Anointing of the Sick. You have received Baptism, Penance, and Holy Eucharist.

In the Bible: John 20:22–23; Luke 22:14–20; John 7:37–39; James 5:14–16; Hebrews 5:1–6; Matthew 19:6
In the Catechism: CCC 1113

65. **Q: What are the Sacraments you can only receive once?**

A: Baptism, Confirmation, and Holy Orders.

In the Bible: Ephesians 4:30
In the Catechism: CCC 1272

**66.** **Q: How is Christian initiation accomplished?**

A: Christian initiation is accomplished with three Sacraments: Baptism which is the beginning of new life; Confirmation which strengthens our new life in Christ; and the Eucharist which nourishes the disciple with Jesus' Body and Blood so that we can be transformed in Christ.

In the Bible: John 3:5; Acts 8:14–17; John 6:51–58
In the Catechism: CCC 1212; 1275

**Going Deeper**

Life is a journey with God. Baptism, Confirmation and First Communion are all great moments in your journey. They are Sacraments that work together to help you live your best life. In Baptism you receive new life in Jesus, in Confirmation God reminds us that he has a special mission for each and every single one of us, and Holy Communion gives us the strength and the wisdom to live that mission by serving God and others.

**67.** **Q: When you were born, did you have Sanctifying Grace (a share in God's life)?**

A: No.

In the Bible: Colossians 1:12–14
In the Catechism: CCC 403, 1250

**68.** **Q: Why are we not born with Sanctifying Grace?**

A: Because we are born with original sin which is the loss of Sanctifying Grace.

In the Bible: Genesis 3:23
In the Catechism: CCC 403, 1250

**69.** **Q: Was any human person conceived without original sin?**

A: Yes, Mary at her Immaculate Conception.

In the Bible: Luke 1:28
In the Catechism: CCC 491, 492

**70.** **Q: What was the original sin?**

A: Adam and Eve were tempted by the devil; and they chose to distrust God's goodness and to disobey his law.

In the Bible: Genesis 3:1–11; Romans 5:19
In the Catechism: CCC 397

**71. Q: Is there really a devil?**

A: Yes.

In the Bible: 1 John 5:19; 1 Peter 5:8
In the Catechism: CCC 391

**72. Q: Is it easier to be bad or to be good?**

A: It is easier to be bad, because original sin has left us with an inclination to sin called concupiscence.

In the Bible: Romans 7:15–18
In the Catechism: CCC 409, 1264, 2516

**73. Q: When did you receive Sanctifying Grace for the first time?**

A: At Baptism.

In the Bible: 2 Corinthians 5:17
In the Catechism: CCC 1265

**74. Q: What is Baptism?**

A: Baptism is the Sacrament of rebirth in Jesus that is necessary for salvation.

In the Bible: 2 Corinthians 5:17; 2 Peter 1:4; Galatians 4:5–7
In the Catechism: CCC 1266, 1277, 1279

**Going Deeper**

Baptism is a great blessing. Through your Baptism you became a member of the Catholic Church. This is another wonderful reason why being Catholic is a great blessing. Through your Baptism, you received new life in Jesus. You were made for mission. God had that mission in mind when you were baptized, and every day since he has been preparing you for your mission. We discover that mission through prayer, the Sacraments, and service to others. God doesn't reveal our mission all at once, he reveals it step-by-step.

**75. Q: What are the fruits of Baptism?**

A: Baptism makes us Christians, cleanses us of original sin and personal sin, and reminds us that we are children of God and members of the Body of Christ—the Church.

In the Bible: Galatians 4:5–7
In the Catechism: CCC 1279

**Going Deeper**

In Baptism God gives us many gifts. We become Christian, our sins are forgiven, we are given new life in Jesus, and God marks us for a great mission. God is able to do this through the power of the Holy Spirit. In Baptism our souls are flooded with the gift of the Holy Spirit, which helps us in our journey to grow closer to God. Each and every Sacrament we receive is full of gifts, big and small. Every blessing reminds us that we are all sons and daughters of a loving Father.

76. **Q: What did Baptism do for you?**

A: It gave me a share in God's life for the first time, made me a child of God, and took away original sin.

In the Bible: 2 Corinthians 5:17; 2 Peter 1:4; Galatians 4:5–7
In the Catechism: CCC 1266, 1279

77. **Q: How old does someone need to be to receive Baptism?**

A: A person can be baptized at any age. Since the earliest times of Christianity, Baptism has been administered to infant children because Baptism is a grace and a gift that is freely given by God and does not presuppose any human merit.

In the Bible: Acts 2:37–39
In the Catechism: CCC 1282

**Going Deeper**

God's love is a free gift. There is nothing you could do to earn or lose God's love. You may be tempted to think that God's love is something to be earned. This is simply not true. God loved you into life, and God loved you into the Church. You did nothing to be born, and if you were baptized as an infant you did nothing to be baptized. You didn't do anything to deserve life or Baptism. God freely gives you life and faith.

78. **Q: Who administers the Sacrament of Baptism?**

A: Anyone can administer the Sacrament of Baptism in an emergency by pouring water over that person's head and saying, "I baptize you in the name of the Father, and of the Son, and of the Holy Spirit." Baptism, however, is usually administered by a priest or deacon.

In the Bible: Matthew 28:19
In the Catechism: CCC 1284

**Going Deeper**

Not everyone is baptized as an infant. Some people don't learn about Jesus until they are adults. But God wants everyone to receive the blessing of Baptism. He wants everyone to be a part of his family—the Catholic Church. He wants everyone to be free from original sin. He wants everyone to have new life in his Son Jesus. He wants everyone to spend eternity with him in heaven.

79. **Q: How long do you remain a child of God?**
A: Forever.

> In the Bible: 1 Peter 1:3–4
> In the Catechism: CCC 1272, 1274

80. **Q: Can you lose a share in God's life after Baptism?**
A: Yes.

> In the Bible: Mark 3:29
> In the Catechism: CCC 1861

81. **Q: Can we lose the new life of grace that God has freely given us?**
A: Yes. The new life of grace can be lost by sin.

> In the Bible:1 Corinthians 6:9; 2 Corinthians 5:19–21; 1 John 1:9
> In the Catechism: CCC 1420

**Going Deeper**

At Baptism we are filled with a very special grace. This grace blesses us with new life and brings us into friendship with God. That new life can be hurt or lost when we sin. When that happens, don't worry because God has given us the blessing of Reconciliation! As long as we are truly sorry for our sins and go to Reconciliation, we can once again experience the fullness of life with God. Reconciliation is a great blessing!

82. **Q: How can you lose Sanctifying Grace (a share in God's life)?**
A: By committing mortal sin.

> In the Bible: Galatians 5:19–21; Romans 1:28–32
> In the Catechism: CCC 1861

83. **Q: Which is the worse sin: venial or mortal?**
A: Mortal (deadly) sin.

In the Bible: 1 John 5:16
In the Catechism: CCC 1855, 1874, 1875

84. Q: **What three things are necessary to commit a mortal sin?**

A: 1. You must disobey God in a serious matter.

2. You must know that it is wrong.

3. You must freely choose to do it anyway.

In the Bible: Mark 10:19; Luke 16:19—31; James 2:10-11
In the Catechism: CCC 1857

85. Q: **What happens to you if you die in a state of mortal sin?**

A: You go to hell.

In the Bible: 1 John 3:14—15; Matthew 25:41—46
In the Catechism: CCC 1035, 1472, 1861, 1874

86. Q: **Is there really a hell?**

A: Yes; it is the place of eternal separation from God.

In the Bible: Isaiah 66:24; Mark 9:47, 48
In the Catechism: CCC 1035

87. Q: **What happens if you die with venial sin on your soul?**

A: You go to purgatory where you are purified and made perfect.

In the Bible: 1 Corinthians 3:14—15; 2 Maccabees 12:45—46
In the Catechism: CCC 1030, 1031, 1472

88. Q: **What happens to the souls in purgatory after their purification?**

A: They go to heaven.

In the Bible: 2 Maccabees 12:45
In the Catechism: CCC 1030

89. Q: **Is there really a heaven?**

A: Yes; it is the place of eternal happiness with God.

In the Bible: 1 John 3:2; 1 Corinthians 13:12; Revelation 22:4—5
In the Catechism: CCC 1023, 1024

90. Q: **Can any sin, no matter how serious, be forgiven?**

A: Yes, any sin, no matter how serious or how many times it is committed can be forgiven.

In the Bible: Matthew 18:21–22
In the Catechism: CCC 982

91.  Q: **What is the primary purpose of the Sacrament of Reconciliation?**

A: The primary purpose of the Sacrament of Reconciliation is the forgiveness of sins committed after Baptism.

In the Bible: Sirach 18:12–13; Sirach 21:1; Acts 26:17–18
In the Catechism: CCC 1421, 1446, 1468

### Going Deeper

Through Baptism we become children of God, are welcomed into a life of grace, and given the promise of heaven.  As we get older, we may do things that harm our relationship with God. But God keeps loving us, and invites us to participate in regular Reconciliation so that our friendship with him can always be as strong as it was in Baptism. If we offend God, the best thing to do is to say sorry to God by going to Reconciliation.

92.  Q: **What other names is the Sacrament of Reconciliation known by?**

A: In different places and different times, the Sacrament of Reconciliation is also called the Sacrament of Conversion, Confession or Penance.

In the Bible: Mark 1:15;  Proverbs 28:13; Acts 3:19; 2 Peter 3:9
In the Catechism: CCC 1423, 1424

### Going Deeper

Jesus loves you and he wants to save you from your sins. He wants to save you because he wants to live in friendship with you on earth and in heaven. He wants to share his joy with you and he wants you to share that joy with others. No matter what name is used, the Sacrament of Reconciliation restores our friendship with God and helps us become the-best-version-of-ourselves, grow in virtue, and live a holy life.

93.  Q: **Is the Sacrament of Reconciliation a blessing?**

A: Yes, it is a great blessing from God.

In the Bible: Psalm 32: 1–2; Romans 4:6–8
In the Catechism: CCC 1468, 1496

94.  Q: **Who commits sins?**

A: All people sin.

In the Bible: Romans 3:23–25; 1 John 1:8–10
In the Catechism: CCC 827

95. Q: How can a mortal sin be forgiven?

A: Through the Sacrament of Reconciliation.

In the Bible: 2 Corinthians 5:20–21
In the Catechism: CCC 1446, 1497

96. Q: What is the ordinary way for someone to be reconciled with God and his Church?

A: The ordinary way for someone to be reconciled with God and his Church is by personally confessing all grave sin to a priest followed by absolution.

In the Bible: John 20:23
In the Catechism: CCC 1497

### Going Deeper

We all stray away from God from time to time. When we do, it is a good time to go to the Sacrament of Reconciliation and say sorry to God. You might be tempted to fall into the trap of thinking that your sin is too big for God to forgive. But, there is nothing you can do that will make God stop loving you. The doors of the Church are always open and God is always willing to forgive us when are sorry. The Sacrament of Reconciliation is a great blessing!

97. Q: What three things must you do in order to receive forgiveness of sin in the Sacrament of Confession?

A: 1. You must be truly sorry for your sins.

2. Confess all mortal sins in kind and number committed since your last confession.

3. You must resolve to amend your life.

In the Bible: Romans 8:17; Romans 3:23–26
In the Catechism: CCC 1448

### Going Deeper

When we sin we become restless and unhappy. God doesn't want us to be restless and unhappy so he invites us to come to Reconciliation so that he can fill us with his joy. There may be times in your life when you feel far from God. But never think that God doesn't want you to return to him. Never think that your sins are greater than God's love. God's love and mercy will always be waiting for you in the Sacrament of Reconciliation.

98. Q: What are the three actions required of us in the Sacrament of Reconciliation?

A: The three actions required of us in the Sacrament of Reconciliation are:

repentance, confession of sins to the priest, and the intention to atone for our sins by performing the penance given by the priest.

In the Bible: 1 John 1:9
In the Catechism: CCC 1491

## Going Deeper

Regular Reconciliation is one of the most powerful ways that God shares his grace and mercy with us. God asks us to be sorry for our sins, confess them out loud to a priest, and do an act of penance so that our friendship with God can be restored and strengthened. The more you go to Reconciliation the more you will come to realize the incredible power of God's grace and mercy in your life.

99. **Q: Who has the power to forgive sin?**

A: Jesus Christ through a Catholic priest.

In the Bible: John 20:23; 2 Corinthians 5:18
In the Catechism: CCC 1461, 1493, 1495

100. **Q: Can the priest talk about your sins with other people?**

A: No. The priest must keep secret all sins confessed to him.

In the Bible: 2 Corinthians 5:18–19
In the Catechism: CCC 1467

## Going Deeper

If you are nervous about going to Confession, it's ok. Being nervous is natural. Just know that the priest is there to help you. He will not think poorly of you because of your sins or tell anyone what they are. Instead, he will be happy that you went to Confession. Remember, the priest is there to encourage you, extend God's love and mercy to you, and to help you grow in virtue.

101. **Q: What is the purpose of penance?**

A: After you have confessed your sins, the priest will propose penance for you to perform. The purpose of these acts of penance is to repair the harm caused by sin and to re-establish the habits of a disciple of Christ.

In the Bible: Luke 19:8; Acts 2:38
In the Catechism: CCC 1459–1460

## Going Deeper

Friendship is beautiful but it is also fragile. God gives us the Sacrament of Reconciliation to heal the pain caused by sin and to repair our friendship with him. When we do our penance we show God that we are truly sorry. Penance helps our souls get healthy again.

102. **Q: How often should you go to Confession?**

A: You should go immediately if you are in a state of mortal sin; otherwise, it is recommended to go once a month because it is highly recommended to confess venial sins. Prior to confession you should carefully examine your conscience.

In the Bible: Acts 3:19; Luke 5:31–32; Jeremiah 31:19
In the Catechism: CCC 1457, 1458

### Going Deeper

God loves healthy relationships and forgiveness is essential to having healthy relationships. Regularly going to God in the Sacrament of Reconciliation and asking for forgiveness is a powerful way to have a fabulous relationship with God. Many of the saints went to Reconciliation every month, some even more often. They knew that going to Confession was the only way to be reconciled to God. They also knew that nothing brought them more joy than having a strong friendship with Jesus.

103. **Q: Does the Sacrament of Reconciliation reconcile us only with God?**

A: No. The Sacrament of Reconciliation reconciles us with God and with the Church.

In the Bible: 1 Corinthians 12:26
In the Catechism: CCC 1422, 1449, 1469

### Going Deeper

God delights in his relationship with you and he delights in your relationship with the Church. Sin makes your soul sick, it hurts other people, and it harms your relationship with God and the Church. When we go to Confession, God forgives us and heals our soul. He also heals our relationship with him and with the Church through the Sacrament of Reconciliation.

104. **Q: How do we experience God's mercy?**

A: We experience God's mercy in the Sacrament of Reconciliation. We also experience God's mercy through the kindness, generosity, and compassion of other people. God's mercy always draws us closer to him. We can also be instruments of God's mercy by exercising the works of mercy with kindness, generosity, and compassion.

In the Bible: Luke 3:11; John 8:11
In the Catechism: CCC 1422, 1449, 2447

### Going Deeper

Sometimes when we do something that is wrong we may be tempted to think that God will not love us anymore. But that is never true. God will always love you because our God is a merciful God. God shows us his mercy by forgiving us, teaching us, and caring for our physical and spiritual needs even when we don't deserve it. He shows us his mercy through the Sacrament of Reconciliation and through the loving actions of other people. God invites you to spread his mercy by forgiving others, praying for others, and caring for those in need.

105. **Q: Where in the Church building is Jesus present in a special way?**

A: In the tabernacle.

In the Bible: Exodus 40:34; Luke 22:19
In the Catechism: CCC 1379

106. **Q: Who is the source of all blessings?**

A: God is the source of all blessings. In the Mass we praise and adore God the Father as the source of every blessing in creation. We also thank God the Father for sending us his Son. Most of all we express our gratitude to God the Father for making us his children.

In the Bible: Luke 1:68–79; Psalm 72:18–19
In the Catechism: CCC 1083, 1110

### Going Deeper

You are blessed in so many ways. But every blessing comes from the very first blessing—life! God has given you life and made you his child. This is an incredible blessing! One of the greatest ways we can show God our gratitude is by going to Mass. By showing up every Sunday and participating in Mass, you show God how thankful you are for everything he has done for you.

107. **Q: True or False.  When you receive Holy Communion, you receive a piece of bread that signifies, symbolizes, or represents Jesus.**

A: False.

In the Bible: Matthew 26:26
In the Catechism: CCC 1374, 1413

**108.** **Q: What do you receive in Holy Communion?**

A: The Body, Blood, Soul, and Divinity of Christ.

In the Bible: 1 Corinthians 11:24 ; John 6: 54–55
In the Catechism: CCC 1374, 1413

**Going Deeper**

Jesus is truly present in the Eucharist. It is not a symbol; it is Jesus. We receive all of Jesus in the Eucharist. Even the tiniest crumb that falls from the wafer contains all of Jesus. The bread and wine become Jesus at the moment of Consecration. This is an incredible moment. In this moment Jesus comes among us once again. Every time you go to Mass, bread and wine are transformed into the Body and Blood of Jesus. You are blessed to be able to receive Jesus in the Eucharist.

**109.** **Q: What is Transubstantiation?**

A: Transubstantiation is when the bread and wine become the Body and Blood of Jesus.

In the Bible: Matthew 26:26; Mark 14:22; Luke 22:19–20
In the Catechism: CCC 1376

**Going Deeper**

God has the power to transform everyone and everything he comes in contact with. Everyday, in every Catholic Church, during every Mass, God transforms ordinary bread and wine into the Body and Blood of Jesus Christ. After receiving Jesus in the Eucharist, many of the saints prayed that they would become what they had received. God answered their prayers and transformed their lives by helping them to live like Jesus. Just like with the saints, God can transform your life. Every time you receive Jesus in the Eucharist worthily, you can become a little more like him. Just like Jesus, you can love generously and serve powerfully everyone you meet.

**110.** **Q: When does the bread and wine change into the Body and Blood of Christ?**

A: It is changed by the words and intention of the priest at the moment of Consecration during Mass. The priest, asking for the help of the Holy Spirit, says the same words Jesus said at the Last Supper: "This is my body which will be given up for you... This is the cup of my blood..."

In the Bible: Mark 14:22; Luke 22:19–20
In the Catechism: CCC 1412, 1413

### Going Deeper

The Last Supper is the most famous meal in the history of the world. In that room two thousand years ago, Jesus gave himself completely to his apostles. Every time we come to Mass, the priest recites the same words as Jesus during the Last Supper. When he does, the wheat bread and grape wine become the Body and Blood of Jesus. Amazing! Jesus wants to give himself completely to you just as he gave himself completely to his apostles at the Last Supper. Jesus wants to be invited into your life. He wants to encourage you, guide you, listen to you, and love you. He offers himself to you in a special way at Mass, especially in the amazing gift of Holy Communion.

111. **Q: What are the benefits of receiving the Body and Blood of Jesus in the Eucharist?**

    A: When you receive Jesus in the Eucharist you become more united with the Lord, your venial sins are forgiven, and you are given grace to avoid grave sins. Receiving Jesus in the Eucharist also increases your love for Jesus and reinforces the fact that you are a member of God's family — the Catholic Church.

    In the Bible: John 6:56–57
    In the Catechism: CCC 1391–1396

### Going Deeper

The Eucharist empowers us to do great things for God. The saints did incredible things for God throughout their lives and the Eucharist was the source of their strength. Through Holy Communion we grow closer to God, move further away from sinful habits, and grow in love for Jesus and the Catholic Church. The Eucharist is the ultimate food for your soul and it will give you the strength and courage to serve God and others powerfully just like the saints.

112. **Q: How important is the Eucharist to the life of the Church?**

    A: The Eucharist is indispensable in the life of the Church. The Eucharist is the heart of the Church. One of the reasons the Eucharist is so important to the life of the Church is because, through it, Jesus unites every member of the Church with his sacrifice on the cross. Every grace that flows from Jesus' suffering, death, and Resurrection comes to us through the Church.

    In the Bible: John 6:51, 54, 56
    In the Catechism: CCC 1324, 1331, 1368, 1407

### Going Deeper

Jesus promised to be with us always, no matter what. He has been keeping this promise for over 2,000 years. Jesus is always with us in the Eucharist. The Eucharist unites us to Jesus and his Church. It also unites us to one another. We are blessed to have the Eucharist. Only through the Catholic Church can we receive the gift of the Eucharist. We are blessed to be Catholic.

113.  Q: **Should you receive Holy Communion in the state of mortal sin?**
      A: No. If you do, you commit the additional mortal sin of sacrilege.

> In the Bible: 1 Corinthians 11:27–29
> In the Catechism: CCC 1385, 1415, 1457

### Going Deeper

If Jesus came to visit your home and it was so messy you couldn't open the door to let Jesus in, that would be terrible. No matter how much Jesus wants to be a part of our lives he will never force himself upon us. Mortal sin slams the door of our souls in Jesus' face. It breaks our relationship with God and prevents the wonderful graces of the Eucharist from flowing into our hearts, minds, and souls. Reconciliation reopens the door to our souls and let's Jesus enter our lives again.

114.  Q: **What is sacrilege?**
      A: It is the abuse of a sacred person, place, or thing.

> In the Bible: 1 Corinthians 11:27–29
> In the Catechism: CCC 2120

115.  Q: **If you are in a state of mortal sin, what should you do before receiving Holy Communion?**
      A: You should go to Confession as soon as possible.

> In the Bible: 2 Corinthians 5:20
> In the Catechism: CCC 1385, 1457

116.  Q: **Who offered the first Mass?**
      A: Jesus Christ.

> In the Bible: Mark 14:22–24
> In the Catechism: CCC 1323

117.  Q: **When did Jesus offer the first Mass?**
      A: On Holy Thursday night, the night before He died, at the Last Supper.

**118. Q: Who offers the Eucharistic sacrifice?**

A: Jesus is the eternal high priest. In the Mass, he offers the Eucharistic sacrifice through the ministry of the priest.

In the Bible: Mark 14:22; Matthew 26:26; Luke 22:19; 1 Corinthians 11:24
In the Catechism: CCC 1348

### Going Deeper

The Last Supper was the first Eucharistic celebration. This was the apostles First Communion, and the first time anybody had ever received the Eucharist. The Mass is not just a symbol of what happened that night. Jesus is truly present in the Eucharist. Every time we receive Holy Communion Jesus gives himself to us in the same way he gave himself to his apostles over 2,000 years ago. Jesus works through the priest at Mass to transform the bread and wine into his Body and Blood.

**119. Q: What is the Sacrifice of the Mass?**

A: It is the sacrifice of Jesus Christ on Calvary, the memorial of Christ's Passover, made present when the priest repeats the words of Consecration spoken by Jesus over the bread and wine at the Last Supper.

In the Bible: Hebrews 7:25–27
In the Catechism: CCC 1364, 1413

### Going Deeper

God loves you so much and he will go to unimaginable lengths to prove his love for you. On Good Friday Jesus was beaten, bullied, mocked, spat upon, cursed at, and crucified on the cross. Jesus laid down his life for us. On Easter Sunday Jesus rose from the dead. He did this so that we might live a very different life while here on earth and happily with him forever in heaven. Every time we go to Mass we remember the life of Jesus, the path he invites us to walk, and the incredible lengths he went to show us his love.

**120. Q: Who can preside at the Eucharist?**

A: Only an ordained priest can preside at the Eucharist and Consecrate the bread and the wine so that they become the Body and Blood of Jesus.

In the Bible: John 13:3–8
In the Catechism: CCC 1411

## Going Deeper

To be a priest is a great honor and privilege. Priests lay down their lives to serve God and his people. The priesthood is a life of service. One of the ultimate privileges of the priesthood is standing in Jesus' place and transforming bread and wine into the Eucharist. This privilege is reserved for priests alone. Nobody other than a priest can do this.

121. **Q: How do we participate in the Sacrifice of the Mass?**

A: By uniting ourselves and our intentions to the bread and wine, offered by the priest, which become Jesus' sacrifice to the Father.

In the Bible: Romans 12:1
In the Catechism: CCC 1407

122. **Q: What does the Eucharistic celebration we participate in at Mass always include?**

A: The Eucharist celebration always includes: the proclamation of the Word of God; thanksgiving to God the Father for all his blessings; the Consecration of the bread and wine; and participation in the liturgical banquet by receiving the Lord's Body and Blood. These elements constitute one single act of worship.

In the Bible: Luke 24:13–35
In the Catechism: CCC 1345–1355, 1408

## Going Deeper

The Mass follows a certain formula that is always repeated and never changes. You could go to Mass anywhere in the world and you will always find it is the same. At every Mass we read from the Bible, show God our gratitude for the blessing of Jesus, witness bread and wine transformed into the Body and Blood of Jesus, and receive Jesus during Holy Communion. In the midst of this great routine, God wants to surprise you. You could spend a lifetime going to Mass every single day and at the end of your life still be surprised by what God has to say to you in the Mass. The Mass is truly amazing!

123. **Q: What role does music play in the Mass?**

A: Sacred music helps us to worship God.

In the Bible: Ps 57:8–10; Ephesians 5:19; Hebrews 2:12; Colossians 3:16
In the Catechism: CCC 1156

## Going Deeper

Sometimes when we are praying it can be difficult to find the right words to express how we feel. To help us, God gives us the great gift of sacred music. Over the course of the Mass there will be songs of praise, songs of worship, songs of petition, and songs of thanksgiving. Sacred music helps raise our hearts to God and bond us together as a community calling out to God with one voice.

124. **Q: What is the Lord's Day?**

A: Sunday is the Lord's Day. It is a day of rest. It is a day to gather as a family. It is the principal day for celebrating the Eucharist because it is the day of the Resurrection.

In the Bible: Exodus 31:15; Matthew 28:1; Mark 16:2; John 20:1;
In the Catechism: CCC 1166; 1193; 2174

**Going Deeper**

Sunday is a very special day. The Resurrection of Jesus is so important that we celebrate it every day at Mass. But we celebrate the Resurrection of Jesus in a special way every Sunday. We do that by resting, spending time with family, and going to Mass. The Lord's Day is a day to marvel at all the amazing ways God has blessed us, and because of that it is a day of gratitude.

125. **Q: Is it a mortal sin for you to miss Mass on Sunday or a Holy Day through your own fault?**

A: Yes.

In the Bible: Exodus 20:8
In the Catechism: CCC 2181

126. **Q: Which person of the Holy Trinity do you receive in Confirmation?**

A: The Holy Spirit.

In the Bible: Romans 8:15
In the Catechism: CCC 1302

127. **Q: What happens in the Sacrament of Confirmation?**

A: The Holy Spirit comes upon us and strengthens us to be soldiers of Christ that we may spread and defend the Catholic faith.

In the Bible: John 14:26; 15:26
In the Catechism: CCC 1303, 2044

128. **Q: What is Confirmation?**

A: Confirmation is a Sacrament that perfects Baptismal grace. Through it we receive the Holy Spirit and are strengthened in grace so we can grow in virtue, live holy lives, and carry out the mission God calls us to.

In the Bible: John 20:22; Acts 2:1–4
In the Catechism: CCC: 1285, 1316

### Going Deeper

When you are older you will be blessed to receive the Sacrament of Confirmation. Confirmation reminds us that in Baptism God blessed us with a special mission and filled us with the Holy Spirit. Through an outpouring of the Holy Spirit at Confirmation, we are filled with the courage and wisdom to live out the mission God has given us. Confirmation deepens our friendship with Jesus and the Catholic Church. It reminds us that we are sons and daughters of a great King. It will be a special moment in your life and a wonderful blessing!

129. **Q: When is Confirmation received?**

A: Most Catholics in the West receive Confirmation during their teenage years, but in the East Confirmation is administered immediately after Baptism.

In the Bible: Hebrews 6:1–3
In the Catechism: CCC 1306, 1318

### Going Deeper

Baptism, Confirmation and First Holy Communion are called the Sacraments of Initiation. In a special way, the Sacraments of Initiation deepen our friendship with Jesus and the Church, fill us with what we need to live out God's mission for our lives, and inspire us to become all that God created us to be. It is important to remember that these three Sacraments are connected. They are the foundation for a fabulous friendship with God on earth and forever in heaven. In some parts of the world, and at different times throughout history, people have received these Sacraments at different times according to local traditions and practical considerations. For example, hundreds of years ago, the bishop may have only visited a village once every two or three years, and so Confirmation would take place when he visited. Even today, some children receive Baptism, First Communion, and Confirmation all at the same time.

130. **Q: What are the Seven Gifts of the Holy Spirit?**

A: Wisdom, understanding, counsel, fortitude, knowledge, piety, and fear of the Lord.

In the Bible: Isaiah 11:2–3
In the Catechism: CCC 1830, 1831

131. Q: **Before you are confirmed, you will promise the bishop that you will never give up the practice of your Catholic faith for anyone or anything. Did you ever make that promise before?**

A: Yes, at Baptism.

In the Bible: Joshua 24:21–22
In the Catechism: CCC 1298

132. Q: **Most of you were baptized as little babies. How could you make that promise?**

A: Our parents and godparents made that promise for us.

In the Bible: Mark 16:16
In the Catechism: CCC 1253

133. Q: **What kind of sin is it to receive Confirmation in the state of mortal sin?**

A: A sacrilege.

In the Bible: 1 Corinthians 11:27–29
In the Catechism: CCC 2120

134. Q: **If you have committed mortal sin, what should you do before receiving Confirmation?**

A: You should make a good Confession.

In the Bible: 2 Corinthians 5:20; Luke 15:18
In the Catechism: CCC 1310

135. Q: **What are the three traditional vocations?**

A: Married life, Holy Orders, and the consecrated life.

In the Bible: Ephesians 5:31–32; Hebrews 5:6, 7:11; Ps 110:4; Matthew 19:12; 1 Corinthians 7:34–66
In the Catechism: CCC 914, 1536, 1601

136. Q: **What are the three vows that a consecrated man or woman takes?**

A: Chastity, Poverty, and Obedience.

In the Bible: Matthew 19:21; Matthew 19:12; 1 Corinthians 7:34–36; Hebrews 10:7
In the Catechism: CCC 915

137. **Q: What are the three ranks (degrees) of Holy Orders?**

A: Deacon, Priest, and Bishop.

In the Bible: 1 Timothy 4:14; 2 Timothy 1:6–7
In the Catechism: CCC 1554

138. **Q: For whom did God make marriage?**

A: One man and one woman.

In the Bible: Genesis 1:26–28; Ephesians 5:31
In the Catechism: CCC 1601, 2360

139. **Q: Is it possible for two men or two women to get married?**

A: No.

In the Bible: Genesis 19:1–29; Romans 1:24–27; 1 Corinthians 6:9
In the Catechism: CCC 2357, 2360

140. **Q: When can a man and woman begin living together?**

A: Only after their marriage.

In the Bible: 1 Corinthians 6:18–20
In the Catechism: CCC 235

141. **Q: What are the three marriage promises a husband and wife make to each other?**

A: Faithfulness, permanence, and being open to having children.

In the Bible: Matthew 19:6; Genesis 1:28
In the Catechism: CCC 1640, 1641, 1664

142. **Q: Why is abortion wrong?**

A: Because it takes the life of a baby in its mother's womb.

In the Bible: Jeremiah 1:5; Psalm 139:13
In the Catechism: CCC 2270

143. **Q: How many commandments are there?**

A: Ten.

In the Bible: Exodus 20:1–18; Deuteronomy 5:6–21
In the Catechism: CCC 2054

144. **Q: What are the Ten Commandments?**

A: 1. 1, the Lord, am your God. You shall not have other gods besides me.
2. You shall not take the name of the Lord, your God, in vain.
3. Remember to keep holy the Lord's Day.
4. Honor your father and mother.
5. You shall not kill.
6. You shall not commit adultery.
7. You shall not steal.
8. You shall not bear false witness against your neighbor.
9. You shall not covet your neighbor's wife.
10. You shall not covet your neighbor's goods.

In the Bible: Exodus 20:1–18; Deuteronomy 5:6–21
In the Catechism: CCC 496, 497

145. **Q: What are the four main kinds of prayer?**

A: The four main kinds of prayer are adoration, thanksgiving, petition, and intercession.

In the Bible: Ps 95:6; Colossians 4:2; James 5:16; 1 John 3:22
In the Catechism: CCC 2628, 2629, 2634, 2638, 2639

146. **Q: How often should we pray?**

A: Every day.

In the Bible: 1 Thessalonians 5:17; Luke 18:1
In the Catechism: CCC 2742

# Acknowledgments

This project began with a dream: to create the best First Reconciliation and
First Communion experience in the world. For the millions of young souls that will
experience this program we hope we have delivered on that dream.

Hundreds of people have poured their time, talent, and expertise into *Blessed*.
It is the result of years of research, development, and testing. To everyone who has
contributed—and you know who you are—in every stage of the process: Thank You!
May God bless you and reward you richly for your generosity.

Special thanks to: Jack Beers, Bridget Eichold, Katie Ferrara, Allen and Anita Hunt,
Steve Lawson, Mark Moore, Shawna Navaro, Father Robert Sherry, and Ben Skudlarek.

Beyond the enormous talent contributions, others have been incredibly generous with
their money. *Blessed* was funded by a group of incredibly generous donors. It will now be
made available at no cost to every parish in North America. This is one of the many ways
that this program is unique.

Everything great in history has been accomplished by people who believed that the
future could be better than the past. Thank you for believing!

Now we offer *Blessed* to the Church as a gift, hopeful that it will help young Catholics
encounter Jesus and discover the genius of Catholicism.

*Blessed* was:

Written by: Matthew Kelly
Illustrated by: Carolina Farias
Designed by: The Dynamic Catholic Design Team
Principal designer: Ben Hawkins

## Help *Blessed* become The-Best-Version-of-Itself

*Blessed* is different from other programs in a hundred ways. One way that it is different is that it is always changing and improving. We need your help with this. Whether you find a typo or think of some fun way to improve the program, please email us and tell us about it so that year after year *Blessed* can become even more dynamic.

**blessed@dynamiccatholic.com**

# Blessed

**The Dynamic Catholic First Communion Experience**
©2017 The Dynamic Catholic Institute and Kakadu, LLC.

ISBN 978-1-942611-61-5

FIRST EDITION

# Mission

{
To re-energize the Catholic Church
in America by developing world-class
resources that inspire people to
rediscover the genius of Catholicism.
}

# Vision

{
To be the innovative leader in the
New Evangelization helping Catholics
and their parishes become
the-best-version-of-themselves.
}

**Dynamic Catholic**
Be Bold. Be Catholic.®

*Blessed* is part of

## THE CATHOLIC MOMENTS SERIES

10 programs we believe will re-energize the Catholic Church in America. If you would like to learn more about The Catholic Moments Series or get involved in our work, visit *DynamicCatholic.com*.

CONFIRMATION

LENT AND EASTER

ADVENT AND CHRISTMAS

FIRST COMMUNION

FIRST RECONCILIATION

MARRIAGE PREP

BIRTH AND BAPTISM

RITE OF CHRISTIAN
INITIATION FOR ADULTS

DAILY PRAYER

SUNDAY MASS

DEATH AND DYING

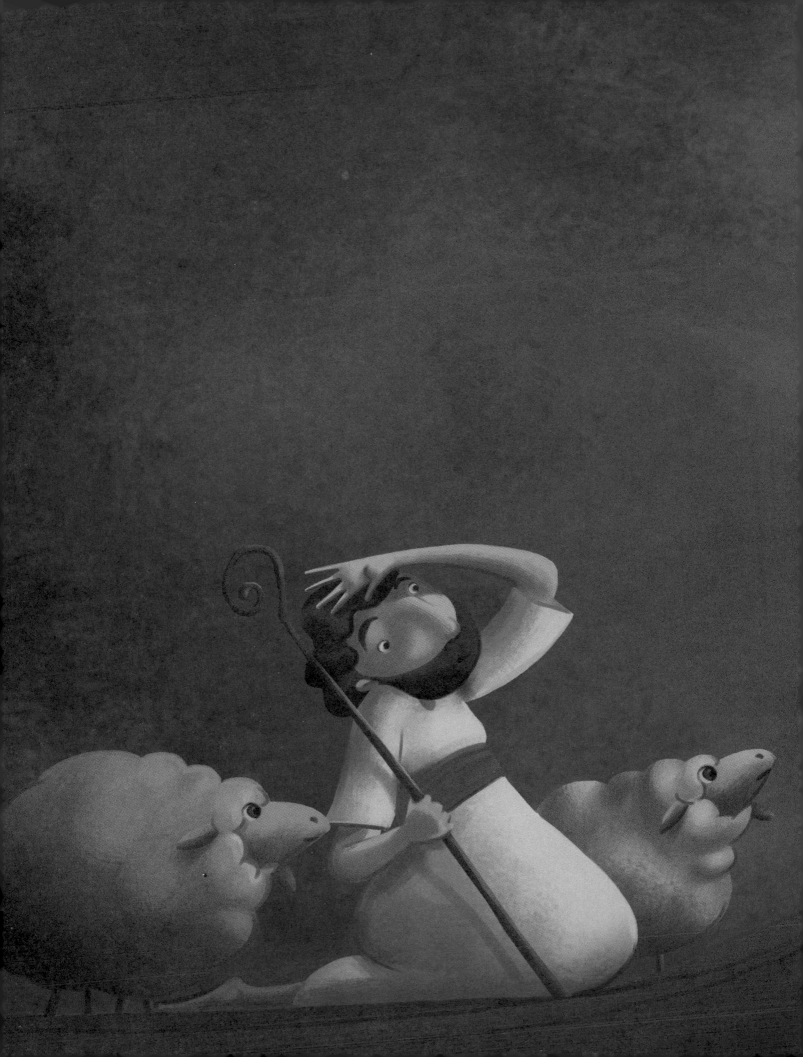